The Library

An Introduction
for
Library Assistants

The Library

An Introduction
for
Library Assistants

Edited by

WILLIAM C. PETRU

Technical Processes Librarian
Hewlett-Packard Company
Palo Alto, California

with the assistance of

MRS. MARTHA W. WEST

Director of Information Services
EDEX Corporation, a subsidiary of Raytheon Company
Mountain View, California

A PROJECT OF THE SAN FRANCISCO BAY REGION CHAPTER

New York   Special Libraries Association

1967

Special Libraries Association was formed in 1909 by librarians of business, professional, governmental and industrial organizations to promote the collection, organization and dissemination of information in specialized fields and to improve the usefulness of special libraries and information services. Its program includes an Annual Convention for the discussion of common problems by experts in various fields of activity; Consultant Services on the organization and administration of special libraries; publication of professional and bibliographical tools; support of a Translations Center that collects and supplies unpublished translations; and a Placement Service for members and employers. Chapters established on a geographical basis and Divisions organized in accordance with subject interest of members implement this program.

Z
670
574

Composition by Vermont Printing Company
Brattleboro, Vermont

Lithoprinted by Edwards Bros.
Ann Arbor, Michigan

Preface

THIS BOOK IS an extensively revised and up-dated version of material originally presented at the Workshops for Library Assistants, sponsored by the San Francisco Bay Region Chapter of Special Libraries Association and held at the University of San Francisco in 1962 and 1964. The purpose of the book is to introduce certain fundamentals of library operations to library assistants, to provide them with a fuller understanding of the goals and procedures of libraries, and to explain the role of the library assistant in his environment.

Emphasis is placed on WHAT library operations are and WHY they exist. It was felt that HOW the operations are performed is better left to each individual library to determine. There is, nonetheless, quite a bit of methodology included here, as it is often inseparable from the what and the why.

Special libraries are treated to a larger degree than other libraries; however, experience from the Workshops has shown that library technicians from special, college, university, and public libraries—ranging from the experienced to the newest of staff members—benefit from the material contained herein. It is hoped that the following chapters on personnel, on types of materials and their acquisition and organization, and on services will prove to be an effective tool for the orientation and training of many more library assistants.

A great deal of work went into developing the original Workshops. The Chapter's Education Committee (Mrs. Margaret Uridge, Chairman), together with the Workshop co-ordinators, the speakers, and the University of San Francisco, shouldered the responsibilities of planning the many details.

In preparing the lectures for publication, the Editor sought—and was freely given—help and advice from many librarians in the San Francisco Bay area. Mrs. Martha West, Chairman of the Chapter's Nonserial Publications Committee, was of great help with a myriad of details. The bibliography, the glossary, and the index are her work. Thanks should also be given to the many library assistants who directly and indirectly contributed to this publication by offering suggestions, by typing manuscripts, and by sharing work loads to permit their librarians time to participate in this effort. Mrs. Darlene Howard is singled out for special thanks.

WILLIAM C. PETRU, Editor
August 1966

Table of Contents

Chapter I

Libraries:
History, Types, Organization, Personnel, and Materials

Mrs. Margaret D. Uridge, Head

General Reference and Interlibrary Borrowing Service
University of California Library, Berkeley, California

THE PURPOSE OF THIS first chapter is to act as an introduction to libraries in general. A brief history of libraries, definitions of the many types of libraries, and a survey of their organization and administration will be covered. The variety of materials found in libraries as well as the personnel who collect, process, and service these materials will be discussed briefly.

The *Encyclopedia Britannica* (1960 ed.) defines a library as follows: "A library (from Lat. *liber*, book) is a collection of printed or written material arranged and organized for the purpose of study and research or of general reading or both. Many libraries also include collections of films, microfilms, phonograph records, lantern slides and the like within the term 'written or printed material'. Libraries may be roughly classified in two ways: by ownership or by use: e.g., national, municipal, county, university, research, school, industrial, club, private, etc.; or by contents; e.g., general, special (including medical, legal, theological, scientific, engineering, etc.)."

Thomas E. Keys, in his *Applied Medical Library Practice,* provides a briefer definition: "A library is a workshop in which tools and materials are in order."

History of Libraries

Long articles on the history of libraries can be found in the major encyclopedias. Briefly, the history of libraries can be said to have begun with a collection of clay tablets found in Babylonia and dating from the 21st century B.C. Libraries existed in the ancient Egyptian temples, and a library in Nineveh dating from about 626 B.C. was the most famous

1

before Greek times. In Greece, private book collections were in existence from the sixth century B.C. on, and the first public library was established during the third century B.C. The most famous libraries of antiquity were those at Alexandria and Pergamum, which contained extensive collections of Greek literature. The first Roman libraries were brought from Greece and Asia Minor.

Continental European and English libraries are the successors of the monastic libraries that preserved learning for the centuries commonly called the Dark Ages. In the 15th century the Vatican Library, the oldest public library in Europe, was formed. The Sorbonne Library in Paris was founded in 1257, and many other great university libraries were opened in the 14th century.

In the United States the first libraries, aside from private libraries, were those organized as subscription libraries. On payment of a membership fee, anyone could belong to these libraries and use their collections. Some of these membership or subscription libraries still exist today. The first public library to be maintained by a unit of local government is said to have been the one founded in Peterborough, New Hampshire, in 1833. A short time later Massachusetts passed the first enabling act allowing a local government to tax its citizenry to support a public library. The establishment of the Boston Public Library provided the impetus for the spread of public libraries in the United States.

Among the outstanding contemporary libraries are the Bibliothèque Nationale in Paris (the national library of France), the British Museum in London (the national library of Great Britain), the Library of Congress in Washington, D. C. (considered the national library of the United States, but not officially designated as such), and large public and university libraries such as the New York Public Library and the libraries of Harvard University.

The history of special libraries is more difficult to summarize than that of public, college, or university libraries. Technically speaking, a monastery library in the Middle Ages, containing chiefly religious works of the period, could be considered a special library—although it would not be thought of as such today. Anthony Kruzas, in *Business and Industrial Libraries in the United States, 1820-1940,* cited 1820 as the beginning date of libraries that are "special" in the sense of the term as employed today. However, as long as universities have had separate subject collections of books, there have been special libraries; as long as there have been associations that have provided their members with a collection of books based on common interests, there have been special libraries. The organization of the Special Libraries Association in 1909 provides a very recent starting point for the modern concept of the special library.

The Library of Congress

The Library of Congress was established in Washington, D. C. in 1800 for the use of members of Congress. When the British burned the Capitol in 1814 and the library was destroyed, the federal government accepted Thomas Jefferson's offer to sell his private library as a nucleus for a new library. Jefferson's collection of books was a "gentleman's library" of over 7,000 volumes and covered many subjects of interest to a well-educated man. Jefferson stipulated that the library be arranged according to his own classification-of-knowledge, and the present Library of Congress classification system has its roots in this early Jeffersonian scheme. During the following 150 years, the Library of Congress has become one of the great national libraries of the world.* It is rivaled in number of items by the Lenin National Library in Moscow, and in subject coverage by the British Museum in London (the national library of Great Britain) and the Bibliothèque Nationale in Paris.

Four points of special interest that may affect the work of almost any library assistant should be emphasized about the Library of Congress:

1. Since the passage of the Copyright Act in 1909, the Library of Congress has been empowered to receive two copies of every book copyrighted in the United States, although it does not have to keep them all. The Library of Congress transfers most of the medical books to the National Library of Medicine (the largest medical library in the world, originally organized as the Library of the Surgeon General of the United States) and the agricultural materials to the National Agricultural Library, which until 1962 was known as the U. S. Department of Agriculture Library.

2. Library of Congress catalog cards are printed and distributed throughout the world either by sale or by deposit. Several research libraries have been designated as depository libraries to receive these cards—familiarly known as L.C. cards. The University of California Library at Berkeley is an example in the West; Harvard University Library, New York State Library, and the University of Michigan Library are further examples of the 17 depositories around the world. Many library assistants are responsible for purchasing L.C. cards for use in cataloging materials in their own libraries. The Library of Congress has issued a *Handbook of Card Distribution,* which explains the various parts of the L.C. card and the procedure for ordering them. More information is given on the construction of catalog cards in Chapter III.

In reality, L.C. cards represent a national cooperative effort in cataloging and classifying books, for they include not only titles cataloged by the Library of Congress for its own use, but also titles cataloged by cooperating libraries in special subject, publishing, or language areas.

3. The National Union Catalog is a Division of the Library of Congress that contains about 16 million cards that record the important hold-

---

* There is a film entitled *Greatest Treasure* (Norwood Studios, 1958, sound, black and white, 16mm) that contains good information on the Library of Congress. It "illustrates the scope of the collections and operations of the Library of Congress and portrays the role of the Library of Congress in the federal government and the life of the nation."

ings of over 700 of the larger and/or specialized libraries in the United States. The holdings of regional union catalogs reflecting the collections of major libraries in areas such as Philadelphia, Denver, and Seattle have been incorporated into the National Union Catalog, as have the entire catalogs of the libraries at Harvard and Yale Universities. Librarians may write to the National Union Catalog for locations of titles of books not found in their immediate areas.

To facilitate spreading information about books, in 1956 the Library of Congress changed the title of its printed book catalog, previously called *Library of Congress: Authors,* to *National Union Catalog: Authors.* This catalog lists books published within the previous five years and contains titles held by an increasing number of cooperating libraries. A fair percentage of the books now found in the *National Union Catalog* are foreign titles not owned by the Library of Congress. This monthly publication, cumulated quarterly and annually, is of great assistance to librarians, not only for locating copies of titles in the United States, but also for verifying bibliographical entries and as an aid in cataloging and classifying such titles. Entries in the printed catalog give the same information found on printed L.C. cards, i.e., a complete bibliographical description of the book, suggested subject and added entries, and classification numbers.

4. The Library of Congress also publishes another cooperative aid for libraries, which is referred to further in Chapter II. *New Serial Titles* is issued monthly and cumulated annually. It also began by listing only new serials added to the Library of Congress, but now lists the holdings of an increasing number of cooperating libraries. It has become, in effect, a continuation of the *Union List of Serials,* 3rd edition, 1966, which covers only periodicals that began publication prior to December 1949. A ten-year cumulation of *New Serial Titles,* 1950-1960, has been issued.

Different Types of Libraries

In the brief historical sketch of libraries, many kinds of libraries were mentioned: private libraries, subscription libraries, national libraries, public libraries, and special libraries. To these should be added school libraries, which are increasing in number and in importance, and the junior college, college, and university libraries.

A few statistics will aid in showing the extent to which libraries have become a part of modern society. Excluding school libraries, the 24th edition of the *American Library Directory,* published in 1964, lists approximately 8,700 public libraries and 2,200 junior college, college, and university libraries. In addition, 485 public libraries of armed forces installations are listed. Anthony Kruzas in *Special Libraries and Information Centers,* 1965, provides statistics on 8,533 specialized library facilities in the United States, including those within colleges and universities, commercial and industrial firms, government agencies, and other organizations such as learned societies, museums, hospitals, and trade associations.

A closer look at these thousands of libraries reveals several ways of grouping them:

GROUPING BY SOURCE OF FINANCIAL SUPPORT

TAX-SUPPORTED: public, county, state, federal government libraries; schools and many colleges and universities.

TUITION-SUPPORTED OR MEMBERSHIP: private schools, colleges and universities; membership libraries, such as the John Crerar Library in Chicago (called a private/public library), and the Mechanics Institute in San Francisco.

INDUSTRIAL AND COMMERCIAL FIRMS: company library facilities that function within the framework of a business operating to produce goods, services or ideas for profit.

ENDOWED INSTITUTIONS (sometimes supplemented by tax support): the Carnegie Endowment for International Peace Library, the Newberry Library in Chicago (another private/public library), and the reference library known as the New York Public Library, which is supported for the use of the public under the Astor, Tilden, Lennox Foundation Endowment; the public-supported part of the library is the branch system.

GROUPING BY PRINCIPAL TYPE OF CLIENTELE

GENERAL PUBLIC: includes the endowed libraries that are for public use and the tax-supported municipal, county, state, and federal government libraries.

STUDENTS: schools, colleges and universities.

INSTITUTION PATIENTS AND INMATES: patients' libraries in hospitals and prison libraries.

INDUSTRIES, BUSINESSES, AND SPECIALIZED STAFF AND CLIENTELE: most special libraries, many specialized government libraries.

GROUPING BY TYPE OF MATERIALS FOUND IN THE LIBRARIES

SUBJECT

General libraries: covering many subjects, this category includes most public, school, university, and college libraries, as well as the large research libraries like the New York Public Library and the Library of Congress.

Specialized subjects: includes the government tax-supported special libraries such as the National Library of Medicine as well as any library that concentrates on limited subject fields. Source of support is not a factor here, as this group includes company libraries, society libraries, or business branches of public libraries.

FORMAT

Books: materials in bound form, such as monographs, texts, bound periodicals. Included in this category are most public libraries and the main libraries of schools, colleges and universities.

Unbound-materials, including periodicals, pamphlets, technical reports, patents, business services: included are most special libraries and the branch or departmental libraries in universities, such as business school libraries.

Non-printed-word materials: music, maps, phonograph records, microforms, motion pictures, tape recordings, photographs, prints and pictures, newspaper clippings, and the like. Libraries having a predominance of these types of materials include broadcasting company libraries, music libraries in schools and universities and music branches of public libraries, U. S. Army Map Service Library, newspaper libraries, picture libraries in advertising agencies, and the Motion Picture Section of the Library of Congress.

Manuscripts: rare-book collections containing incunabula or materials produced prior to the printing press, and the more contemporary manuscripts and typescripts that are in the National Archives in Washington and in the archives of universities and companies, as well as other large research libraries.

Special Libraries

The Special Libraries Association in 1958 defined a special library as follows: "Special library, wherever used in membership requirements, shall be defined as a collection of information materials, maintained by an individual, corporation, association, governmental agency, or any other organized group, and primarily devoted to a special subject and offering specialized service to a specialized clientele. Special subject departments of universities and public libraries and of the Library of Congress shall be considered special libraries."

This seems to overwork the word "special"; however in *Webster's New International Dictionary,* 2nd edition, many of the definitions of the word "special" are appropriate in describing a special library, e.g., "designed or selected for a particular purpose, confined to a definite field of action; specialized, limited, having an individual character" and giving service that is "additional or extra" to regular library service. Herman Henkle, Executive Director of the John Crerar Library in Chicago, said in the prefatory article to the October 1952 *Library Trends* that the services making a library "special" are those services in which "a librarian does some of the reader's work for him . . . and when the primary part of the librarian's job is this, he is a special librarian, regardless of subject or type of library."

Special libraries fall into all the groupings previously mentioned—type of support, type of primary clientele, and type of materials handled. But special libraries are usually considered to be selective rather than general in regard to these groupings:

1. They may be tax-supported but selective in subject coverage, as with the National Library of Agriculture.

6

2. They may be open to the general public but selective in materials, subject, and/or format, as the music branch of a public library.

3. They may be selective in primary clientele as well as subject, such as the Pacific Gas and Electric Company Library or the Atomic Energy Commission Library at Oak Ridge, which requires its users to have security clearance. Selectiveness of clientele is also found in patient and hospital libraries, although their subject matter is general.

Organization of Libraries

Generally, all libraries are responsible to a higher governing body. School, college, and university libraries are one of the educational tools of an institution just like the laboratories within these schools. The large endowed "private-public" libraries, such as the Newberry Library, are administered by a board of trustees for the use of the public. Public municipal, county, state and federal government libraries are part of a governmental organization and as such must fit into their fiscal and administrative pattern. Industrial and commercial libraries must also fit into the larger administrative patterns of their organizations, as must research libraries within government-contract supported organizations, such as the California Institute of Technology Jet Propulsion Laboratory.

A special library, which is part of a larger organization, must follow the procedures governing the larger organization in personnel practices, in purchasing policies, and in fiscal matters. Because so many special libraries are comparatively small units without policies of their own making, it is sometimes felt that special librarians do not need administrative training, that there is no common administrative basis for special libraries, and that special libraries are totally controlled by the variety of commercial, indstrial, research, and association administrative organizations of which they are a part. This is only partially true. Every special librarian must know well the organization that he serves and is a part of, just as a good municipal librarian knows well the community he serves and is a part of. But within the library unit itself, there are certain fundamentals of library administration, library principles, and library procedures that are common to the majority of special libraries, just as they are common to the majority of general libraries.

A special library can be more flexible, more imaginative, and more inventive than other libraries in fulfilling its functions—and special libraries usually are. Because they are often part of the business world with its competitive pressures, speed of service is of greater importance than in more general libraries. The tempo of work in industrial libraries is rapid. Thus, staffs of this type of special library feel themselves part of the "hum" of industry as they contribute their part to the product, the research, or the particular service that their organization as a whole produces.

Library Personnel

The *Objectives and Standards for Special Libraries,* published by Special Libraries Association in 1964, states that "the special library must have at least one professionally qualified librarian and one clerical worker." The standards go on to state that "the recommended ratio of nonprofessional staff to professional staff is three to two." This ratio is not meant to include only professional librarians and nonprofessional clerks. Instead, professional workers include other specialists such as literature searchers who are subject specialists, translators, abstractors and indexers, and perhaps technical writers and editors. Nonprofessional workers include not only clerks but secretaries, stenographers, and general library assistants. The latter are sometimes termed "subprofessionals" or "library technicians," since they require more library knowledge than the usual nonprofessional but less knowledge than a professional librarian.

All library staff members represent the library and the parent organization when they come in contact with the library's clientele—whether in person, by telephone, or in correspondence.

The library-school trained professional should know the American Library Association's *Code of Ethics,* the preamble of which reads, "The library as an institution exists for the benefit of a given constituency, whether it be the citizens of a community, members of an educational institution, or some larger or more specialized group."

Each staff member should also be familiar with the fundamental code of conduct governing any service organization. Remembering the kind of service one would want oneself should be sufficient to guide the personal conduct of members of the library staff, i.e., the need to be competent, well-groomed, attentive personnel who are friendly, alert, and courteous.

Library Materials

THE BOOK

Beside considering the subject matter contained in a book or its rarity due to uniqueness, age, or having belonged to a famous person (which creates value by "association"), there are two fundamental ways to look at the book: *1)* how a book is put together bibliographically, and *2)* how a book is put together physically. These points will be treated again in Chapter III, "The Organization of Library Materials," when catalog cards and the information they contain are described.

BIBLIOGRAPHICAL COMPONENTS

Frontispiece: An illustration or portrait found facing the title page and often meant as a pictorial "key" to the contents. As with illustrations in general, it is not found in all books.

Half-title: The short title of a book appearing alone on a separate page preceding the text or a section of the text. It frequently precedes the title page, and sometimes carries bibliographic information such as series notes.

Title page: The identifying page giving the title of the book, the author, edition, publisher, place, and date of publication. The title page is the most essential page for the cataloger.

Copyright page: The verso (reverse side) of the title page, giving the date of copyright and by whom it was copyrighted. Foreign books also often give the number of copies printed and other information. The Library of Congress catalog card number, by which cards are ordered from the Library of Congress, is found here.

Dedication page: The page following the title page where the author names the person or persons to whom he dedicates the book. Not always used.

Preface or *Foreword:* Here the author acknowledges the assistance received in preparation of the book, including copyright permission. It often tells why the book was written or contains similar explanatory information.

Table of contents: Lists the chapters and other parts of the book and the pages upon which they begin. Tables of contents can sometimes be quite detailed so that by scanning it one obtains a general idea of what the book includes.

Lists of illustrations, maps or plates: Important illustrative material can be listed separately, arranged in the order of their appearance in the book and providing page numbers or the facing-page number in the case of plates.

Plates: Full-page inserted illustrations, frequently on high-gloss paper. Ordinarily plates are not included as numbered pages.

Introduction: Technically, has a purpose different from the preface or foreword. The introduction generally states what the book is about and sometimes acts as a summary of the contents.

Text: The main portion, the body of the book.

Appendix: A section coming after the text, often containing substantiating documents or materials referred to in the text, such as statistical data, questionnaire forms, reprinted documents, and the like. Not always found.

Bibliography: A listing of the important references used or referred to in the text. Sometimes it consists of "recommended reading" for further research into the subject.

Index: An alphabetical list of the important topics, terms, and names found in the book. In scientific and technical books and books designed for reference use, a good index is essential and often is an indication of how carefully the book has been prepared. In evaluating books, librarians often buy or reject materials on the basis of the adequacy of the indexes.

PHYSICAL COMPONENTS

A book is made of paper, glue, thread, and a binding. Each part of the book has a technical name, which is essential to know in describing damage done to a book or discussing binding or mending with a bookbinder.

Cover or *Casing:* This represents the front and back covers and may be boards covered with cloth (as in "bound" books) or heavy paper (as in "paper-backs").

Spine: The back edge that shows when a book stands on the shelf. It is usually on the spine that the call-number of a book is written.

Hinges: The cloth strips that hold the covers to the body of the book. Often the place where damage is first done, requiring rebinding or replacement of the hinges.

End-papers: The lining papers on the inside of the covers that conceal the hinges and seams of the cloth covering. Sometimes they are decorated or contain maps or other illustrative material.

Fly-leaf: A blank page that protects the title page or the first page of text.

Stitching: The sewing holding the sections of the body together.

Leaves (leaf), *pages,* and *signatures:* There are two *pages* on one *leaf,* printed on the recto (front) and verso (back). Several leaves make one signature, which is made by folding one large sheet of printing paper. The terms often used in describing the size of a book, i.e., folio, quarto,

Parts of a Book

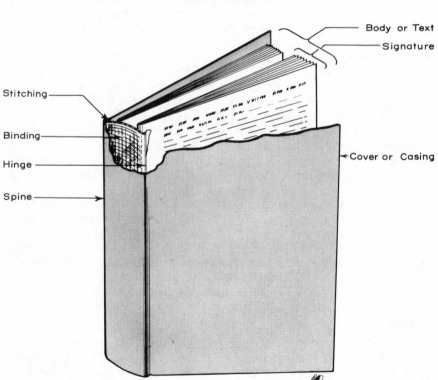

octavo, 12mo, etc., refer to the number of times a large printing-sheet was folded to make a signature of printed leaves. For example, a folio is a large sheet folded once, producing two leaves, with four pages; a quarto is the sheet folded twice (a folio folded once) producing 4 leaves; an octavo is a sheet folded three times, producing 8 leaves.

There are more terms that a binder or a rare-book collector uses in describing books, but the above definitions are the more common ones most likely to be encountered in day-to-day library work.

The proper method of first opening a new book should also be mentioned. First, place the book on its spine and open the front and back covers. Press each cover down on the hinges. Release about ten pages from the front of the book and press down on the inner margin or gutter, as it is called. Do the same from the back of the book. Continue this procedure, alternating front and back, until the center of the book is reached. By doing this carefully and firmly, neither the stitching nor the glue on the spine will be broken or cracked.

DEFINITIONS OF LIBRARY MATERIALS

In describing library materials it is necessary to have definitions relating to their bibliographical and physical forms. Saying that a library has a collection of "books, magazines, and pamphlets" indicates only in the most general terms the contents of a library. A book could in reality be a bound periodical; a magazine could be more properly called a journal; a pamphlet may actually be a patent. It is important to call library items by their proper names to avoid confusion, and the following list of definitions will help in providing bibliographic and physical identification.

MONOGRAPH

A systematic and complete treatise on a particular subject, usually detailed in treatment but not extensive in scope. A monograph is thought of as a bibliographical entity, a book. Physically it may be in one or more volumes. Many book collections in special libraries consist of monographs.

SERIAL

A publication issued in successive parts, usually at regular intervals, and intended to be continued indefinitely. The term serial is an inclusive term covering periodicals (or magazines), newspapers, annuals, and the like and should not be confused with "series." Serials can be hard-bound or soft-bound.

Periodical: A publication with a distinctive title intended to appear in successive (usually unbound) numbers or parts at stated or regular intervals and, as a rule, for an indefinite time. Each part generally contains articles by several contributors. Commonly called magazines, but periodicals is the better term.

Journal: A periodical, specifically a periodical issued by an institution, corporation, or learned society, and containing current news and reports of activities and work in a particular field.

Newspaper: A publication issued at stated and frequent intervals, usually daily, weekly, or semi-weekly, which reports events and discusses topics of current public interest.

Series: A number of separate works, usually related to one another in subject or purpose, issued in succession, normally by the same publisher and in uniform style, with a collective title that generally appears at the head of the title page, on the half-title, or on the cover. A second meaning is several successive volumes of a periodical or other serial publication that are numbered separately to distinguish them from preceding or following volumes of the same publication, e.g., 1st and 2nd series.

OTHER USUALLY UNBOUND MATERIALS

Pamphlet: In a restricted technical sense, an independent publication consisting of a few leaves of printed matter stitched or stapled together but not bound; usually enclosed in paper covers. While independent in the sense that each pamphlet is complete in itself, it is a common custom to issue pamphlets in series, usually numbered consecutively. From a binder's point of view, a pamphlet is any collection of leaves, paper-bound or self-covered, consisting of 64 pages or less.

Report: A publication giving an official or formal record, as of some special investigation, of the activities of a corporate body or of the proceedings of a governmental body. A *technical report,* which is now frequently encountered in special libraries, is a record of the current status of scientific research and development, often funded by a federal agency.

Off-Print: An impression of an article, chapter, or other portion of a larger work, printed from the type or plates of the original and separately issued, sometimes with one or more additional pages or leaves. Called also *separate* or *reprint.*

Patent: An official government publication containing specifications of an invention, such as a machine, a process, an art, or a design.

Non-Commercial (or non-published) publications: Material published as a secondary non-profit activity by an organization. They are often ephemeral in nature, being reproduced in less expensive ways, usually of limited distribution, often for internal use only. Frequently not listed in trade or general bibliographies and soon out of print. Annual business reports and trade catalogs are examples.

SUPPLIES

Non-bibliographic materials that a library must be concerned with are the library supplies. These vary from the regular clerical supplies, e.g., typing paper and erasers, to the specialized supplies produced just for libraries, e.g., library furniture and card catalogs. There are many library-supply houses that specialize in forms, furniture, and aids to libraries. There are too many suppliers available throughout the country to list here; however, a good source for such information is the buyer's guide published each April 1 in *Library Journal.* This buyer's guide is also published in the *Bowker Annual,* a yearbook of library and book trade statistics and other useful information.

Library of Congress cards should be considered as another form of library supplies. They represent, as stated earlier, the product of cooperative cataloging and may be purchased from the Card Division of the Library of Congress by following the rules set down in *Instructions for Ordering Library of Congress Printed Cards,* available from the Card Division. Many libraries have designated one sheet of their multiple-order forms as a Library of Congress card order form, as discussed further in Chapter II.

Recommended Reading

ASHWORTH, Wilfred, ed. *Handbook of Special Librarianship and Information Work.* London: ASLIB, 1965. 387 p.

KEYS, Thomas Edward. *Applied Medical Library Practice.* With chapters by Catherine Kennedy [and] Ruth M. Tews. Springfield, Ill.: Thomas, [1958]. xix, 495 p.

KRUZAS, Anthony Thomas. *Business and Industrial Libraries in the United States, 1820-1940.* New York: Special Libraries Association, 1965. 133 p.

LA MONTAGNE, Leo E. *American Library Classification, with Special Reference to the Library of Congress.* Hamden, Conn.: Shoe String Press, 1961. x, 433 p.

MEDICAL LIBRARY ASSOCIATION. *Handbook of Medical Library Practice, with a Bibliography of the Reference Works and Histories in Medicine and the Allied Sciences,* 2nd ed., rev. & enl. Chicago: American Library Association, 1956. xv, 601 p. Out of print; new edition in preparation.

SPECIAL LIBRARIES ASSOCIATION. *Personnel Survey 1959.* [New York: Special Libraries Association, c1960.] 24 p. Reprinted from *Special Libraries,* vol. 51, no. 3, March 1960.

STEINKE, Eleanor G. Orientation and Training for the Non-Professional Library Staff. *Medical Library Association Bulletin,* vol. 50, no. 1, January 1962, p. 36-41.

STRAUSS, Lucille (Jackson). *Scientific and Technical Libraries: Their Organization and Administration.* New York: Interscience, 1964. xi, 398 p. Revision of *Technical Libraries: Their Organization and Management,* published in 1951 by Special Libraries Association.

Chapter II

Acquisition of Library Materials

Mrs. Charlotte G. Owens, Supervisor

Books Technical Services
Lockheed Missiles and Space Company, Palo Alto, California

The Acquisition Process

SCOPE AND CHARACTER

WHY does the library profession use the word acquisition instead of a simpler term such as ordering or order work? *Webster's Unabridged Dictionary*, 3rd edition, defines acquisition as: "*1)* the act or action of acquiring and, *2)* a thing acquired or gained." These definitions fit the library activity accurately because libraries don't always order or place an order. Sometimes they acquire materials as gifts, sometimes on an exchange basis, and sometimes on an interlibrary loan from another library.

There are certain broad principles all libraries follow in varying degrees in their acquiring. The details as to how acquiring is done differ from library to library, because acquisition policies depend on the organization of the library, on the rules, regulations, and restrictions of the purchasing office, and on the general operating procedures of the organization.

Knowing how an acquisitions department is related to the other departments of a library is of prime importance for working effectively. The staff of all other departments depend upon the acquisitions department, whether it is a cataloger who must have materials to catalog, a circulation librarian who must have books to circulate, or a reference librarian who must have materials in which to find answers to the many questions asked.

TYPES OF MATERIALS ACQUIRED

Generally it is thought that libraries acquire only books and periodicals. However, special libraries particularly must deal with materials that take many other forms. Following is a list of some of the more common types: books, periodicals, government publications, both state and federal, maps, translations, technical reports, reprints, patents, preprints, pamphlets, and pictures. Each of these will be discussed further in the sections below.

Selection

A good library collection is determined by the decisions governing the selection of materials. Strength of the collection is measured by its ability to meet the needs of a library's clientele and not on numbers of items included in the collection.

CRITERIA FOR SELECTION

Librarians try to select carefully and with judgment. The criteria to bear in mind are: 1) the fields of interest of the library's clientele, and 2) the intellectual level of the library's clientele.

These criteria should be applied in a public library, or a school library, or a special library. In a public library, selection often depends on the library's location. Is it in an area where well-educated, sophisticated users live and work, or is the area one of low-income families who want self-education and how-to-do-it literature? A dominant religious group in the community served influences book selection, and in a school library the collection is strongly determined by what courses are taught, what types of material are on reading lists, and what the reading levels of the students are. In a special library it is necessary to know in what fields research is taking place, what new product lines are being brought out, or what the latest marketing surveys reveal.

At the same time that interests are being served, the level of that interest is also important. Will an introductory text be sufficient, or does a reader require deeper coverage? Frequently a well-rounded collection needs a balance of both scholarly and introductory-type literature to provide for a scholar wishing to know a little about another field or to serve as "memory-refresher" texts.

SOURCES FOR SELECTION

The establishment of a library will not be discussed here but rather the selection tools that are used.

BOOKS

Probably the most widely used selection tool is the periodical entitled *Publishers' Weekly*, published by the R. R. Bowker Company in New York City. Each issue has news about the publishing field and contains an author listing of titles published that week, with a very concise note as to contents. Publisher, price, Dewey Decimal Classification, Library of Congress Classification, and L.C. card number are given. Some pamphlet material is also listed. There are also advertisements for new books, plus all sorts of interesting news notes about the publishing and book trade.

Seasonal announcement numbers of new books to be published are issued four times a year. Each month the "Weekly Record" entries in *Publishers' Weekly* are cumulated by Dewey Decimal arrangement in a separate publication, the *American Book Publishing Record.*

The *Library Journal,* also published by Bowker, is a professional journal listing new books and reviewing a large number of them. Certain issues are devoted to listing titles in specified subject fields, such as business books, technical books, and religious books. Longer, more evaluative descriptions of the contents of each book are given. Both *Publishers' Weekly* and *Library Journal* cover titles in all fields of interest.

In addition to these two general selection tools, there are many current lists of new titles in specified subject areas—technology, medicine, economics, and the like. Most libraries subscribe to those that cover their subject areas of interest.

Another method of selection is to scan bibliographies on specified subjects. These listings include older materials. References selected from these sources are generally recommended by a library user who is a subject specialist trained to keep up with the literature in his field. Accepting recommendations of this sort is an excellent way to become aware of good material for the collection. It is usually a sign that the library is performing its selection job well when a recommended book is on order or already in the collection.

Further selection tools are publishers' catalogs, both foreign and domestic. Every publisher issues a new catalog each year, which is generally arranged by subject, author, and title. Sometimes short descriptive notes are included. It is well to remember that a publisher is selling books and anything he publishes will be described in the best possible light. Occasionally publishers representatives will call to discuss their new titles, permitting an examination of the contents of books. Representatives call on public and school librarians more often than on special librarians, because a wider range of books can be shown to the former than to the latter.

Publishers also send out blurbs, which are ordinarily single-page advertisments. Scanning blurbs is a good method of keeping aware of what new titles are being published, but one must be cautious for sometimes new blurbs are distributed about older books.

A source of good book reviews are subject journals. Sometimes these reviews are signed, meaning that a specialist was solicited to write the review. Scanning special journals for reviews is time-consuming but worthwhile since library users often learn about new titles they request for purchase from these sources.

Although they are not as current as the subject journals, there are two monthly publications that are excellent sources for technical books. *Technical Book Review Index,* published by the Special Libraries Association, is best described by quoting from its statement of purpose: " . . . to identify reviews in current scientific, technical, and trade journals and to quote from these reviews. In this evaluation of scientific and technical books, reviews constitute the best existing source of information." *New Technical Books* originates from the New York Public Library and is actually its accessions list. Instead of reviews, this publication lists the tables of contents of books with short descriptive annotations of scope of material, for whom intended, and similar statements.

PERIODICALS

Current periodical subscriptions and periodical collections of back-files are frequently of greater importance in a special library than the book collection. Current issues carry information that has not been published in book form, and back issues may contain information that has never been published in book form. Main sources for both selecting and identifying periodicals are described below:

Directory of Newspapers and Periodicals issued by N. W. Ayer and Sons: This is not a selective list, nor is there any description aside from a few words on the subject contents of the entries. Complete order information is given, and there is a broad subject index. Ayers, as it is commonly called, covers only publications issued in the United States and Canada.

Ulrich's International Periodicals Directory: The arrangement is by subject, with index by title, to the best known periodicals of the world, including an extensive coverage of countries behind the Iron Curtain. The latest edition is in two volumes, with volume I being devoted to science, technology, and medicine, and volume II to the arts, humanities, social science and business.

Standard Periodical Directory: Subject-arranged, this directory includes —in addition to regular magazines and journals—newsletters, government publications, house organs, advisory services, directories, serials, comic books, transactions and proceedings of professional societies, and yearbooks.

The best method of keeping up with new periodicals is through *New Serial Titles,* published by the Library of Congress. This monthly publication is arranged by title and cumulates annually; the annual volumes are also cumulated at intervals. To aid selection, there is also a classed-subject arrangement published in 12 monthly issues without a cumulation, but no descriptions of the new journals on which to base an evaluation are given; however, as an announcement medium, *New Serial Titles* is effective.

Journals in special subject fields frequently announce new periodical titles in that field and sometimes provide a review or more information about the new title.

Publishers of periodicals also annouce new journals by direct mailings, the same way new books are announced.

GOVERNMENT DOCUMENTS

Government documents can be selected from the *Monthly Catalog of United States Government Publications,* published by the Superintendent of Documents, U. S. Government Printing Office. An index is included each month with entries appearing under subject or title. At intervals the Superintendent of Documents sends out announcements about new and old titles in a listing called *Selected United States Government Publications,* which can be requested without charge from the Government Printing Office.

State documents are generally listed in serial publications originating from a state agency, which is usually the principal depository of such publications. For example, the California State Library issues a monthly listing entitled *California State Publications;* the Michigan State Library does the same for that state. In Florida, the University of Florida Libraries issues the *Short Title Checklist of Official Publications.* In Minnesota, the state Documents Section publishes a list. These free or inexpensive lists are as invaluable for state documents as is the *Monthly Catalog* for federal documents, and every library should have them.

Another source of information on state documents is the *Monthly Checklist of State Publications,* which gives cataloging data on state publications received by the Library of Congress.

TECHNICAL REPORTS

Within the past few years there has been a great increase of the form of literature called the technical report. It is usually a paper-backed, stapled or spiral-bound report on the current status of some research project, frequently sponsored by (but not necessarily done by) an agency of the federal government. A great deal of the work reported has direct bearing on the national defense of the United States, and for this reason the acquisition and handling of much of the technical report literature is governed by strict regulations. To attempt to reduce these rules to an intelligent, meaningful summary within this introduction to libraries is not feasible, so only generalities will be covered here. If further information is needed on technical reports, Special Libraries Association has published *Dictionary of Report Series Codes,* which contains a good introduction to this type of material and several references for further reading.

There are two main sources for unclassified technical reports available to the general public: the Government Printing Office (GPO), and the Clearinghouse for Federal Scientific and Technical Information (CFSTI). The *Monthly Catalog* lists technical reports available from GPO, while the CFSTI issues *Government-wide Index to Federal Research & Development Reports* as an announcement medium. Since prices are indicated, both catalogs are necessary purchasing tools as well as selection tools. Both agencies operate on a cash-in-advance basis for material ordered from them (GPO also sells coupons). For organizations that do frequent ordering, deposit accounts can be set up with each agency.

TRANSLATIONS

Translations can be selected from lists published by firms dealing in translations. Much valuable technical foreign material can be acquired in this way. The Associated Technical Services in East Orange, New Jersey, and Consultants Bureau and Plenum Press in New York City publish regular lists of their translations, and any library can be placed on their mailing list. Henry Brutcher in Altadena, California, is another commercial translator who publishes a monthly list of translations for sale. There are others.

The Clearinghouse for Federal Scientific and Technical Information in Springfield, Virginia, publishes a semi-monthly list entitled *Technical Translations,* which includes translations from domestic and foreign government agencies, commercial publishers, and those available from the Special Libraries Association Translations Center, which is housed at the John Crerar Library in Chicago. To accomplish its aims of being a national depository for translations and providing information about them, the Center acquires unpublished translations from voluntary contributors and provides copies to others who need them, or information on the sources of translations if they are not represented in the Center's files. Translations in *Technical Translations* are listed by subject with order information given.

In the field of science and technology, translated material is of prime importance, particularly Russian translations. More and more Russian journals are being translated into English and to discover what these are, consult the Library of Congress publication, *List of Russian Serials Being Translated into English and Other Western Languages.* Subject-arranged, each translated title gives the L.C. number, frequency, issue that has been translated, and publisher of translation. The list is free from the Library of Congress, Reference Department, Science and Technology Division. *Technical Translations* also occasionally publishes lists of cover-to-cover translated journals.

PAMPHLETS

Pamphlet material varies in importance from library to library. Since many pamphlets can be judged ephemeral (of short-time importance) it is desirable to have a routine weeding* procedure. This, however, is a time-consuming luxury not many libraries can afford. Pamphlet material can be very timely and contain up-to-date information, but source indexes for this type of library material are not good. The *Vertical File Index* is of some use, as is the *Public Affairs Information Service.* The *Publishers' Weekly* "Weekly Record" also includes some pamphlet material.

PATENTS

Patents are generally acquired from the U. S. Patent Office in Washington, D. C. The weekly *Official Gazette of the U. S. Patent Office* is the principal source for selecting patents in all subject fields.

---

* "Weeding" in library jargon is the selective discarding of library materials, based on the evaluation of each item for currentness, present need, availability of subject content in other forms, historical value, past usage, and other criteria that each library determines for itself.

REPRINTS AND PREPRINTS

Reprints are singly reprinted articles from periodicals. These are acquired from the publisher or author. Frequently periodical articles reproduced on photocopy equipment are also termed as reprints. Reproducing articles is an important aspect of library service, since this material is generally bound into a volume covering many issues of a periodical. Instead of allowing whole bound volumes of periodicals to leave the library for perhaps extended lengths of time, the few pages needed are reproduced. Since periodicals are copyrighted just as books are, care must be taken to keep this form of reproduction to a minimum. Further information on photocopying is found in Chapter IV.

Preprints are advanced copies of papers given at conferences and symposia. They can be purchased from the publishers (usually the society or association sponsoring the conference), but in many instances a library will set up a standing order to receive all preprints of certain regularly held conferences in the field of interest of the library's clientele. Conference announcements generally tell how preprints may be ordered. Preprints are another source of not-yet-formally-published information and are generally in heavy demand.

While preprints are issued before a conference, transactions and proceedings are issued after a conference. These materials, too, are generally popular, and many proceedings are published in permanent book form. An excellent selection aid for this type of material is *Proceedings in Print,* a bimonthly publication indexing by subject, editor, title, and sponsoring society recent conference proceedings in science, technology, and medicine.

Two other sources that aid in identifying meetings from which preprints and reprints might be of interest are *Scientific Meetings* and *Technical Meetings Index.* The former is a three-times-a-year publication of the Special Libraries Association and covers scientific, technical, medical, health, engineering, management organizations, and university and colleges that are sponsoring future national, international, and regional meetings, symposia, colloquia, and institutes. The latter is a quarterly publication of the Technical Meetings Index Service in New Hartford, New York. United States and Canadian meetings only are covered in the fields of aerospace, physical sciences, engineering, pharmaco-medicine, chemistry, life sciences, and agriculture.

PICTURES AND MAPS

Pictures and maps can be important items in history, art, or geology libraries. The Special Libraries Association's book *Picture Sources* provides a good selection aid for this type of material, while map publishers' catalogs, U. S. Coast and Geodetic Survey indexes, and U. S. Aeronautical Chart and Information Center indexes are all good sources for map information.

Ordering Procedures

VERIFICATION

For the actual ordering of material, it is first necessary to have complete order information, which at a minimum includes author, first name or initials, complete title, publisher, date, and price. Obtaining this information is called verification. When a title is selected for purchase from one of the sources previously discussed, usually all of this information is given. However, a reader requesting a title may not have complete ordering data.

Books in Print, published by R. R. Bowker, is an excellent place to start verifying a title. This is an annual author and title list of all books in print published by American publishers. A companion volume is the *Subject Guide to Books in Print.* Publishers' catalogs are also useful for verifying data. *Cumulative Book Index* can be checked for older titles and for new titles after *Books in Print* goes to press. This is a monthly world list of books in the English language, with quarterly, semi-annual, annual, two-year, and five-year cumulations. It is arranged by subject, author, and title and is a basic tool for any acquisitions department.

Periodicals can be verified through cumulations of the *Union List of Serials, Ulrich's* or *Ayers,* which were all discussed earlier. Government documents can be verified through the *Monthly Catalog of United States Government Publications.* It is important to verify government documents, because requests for this type of literature are likely to be the most sketchy. If orders are sent to the Government Printing Office with incomplete information, sometimes the order will not be filled or considerable time will be taken in so doing. A government document order, state or federal, should include along with other order information the document catalog number identifying the particular title. Sometimes in verifying a title from the *Monthly Catalog* or a state listing, it is learned that the document cannot be purchased as it is for official use only or that other limitations on distribution have been set. Using the *Monthly Catalog* intelligently is of the utmost importance, for special libraries particularly.

Sending dealers accurate order information is an important part of the acquisitions department's job. A title ordered with insufficient information or misinformation slows up the entire ordering process.

WHERE TO BUY

BOOKS

Once the library knows what it wants to acquire, an order is sent to the publisher of the material or to a middle-man who is called a jobber. A book jobber is different from a corner bookstore in that he is a wholesaler, i.e., he sells his wares to book stores and libraries at a discount, and he carries many publishers' titles.

Best service is obtained by using a jobber for most of a library's material, rather than going directly to publishers. First, publishers prefer that libraries deal with jobbers since they do not want to handle many small, single-title orders. Second, a library would spend far too much time writing individual orders to many publishers and paying with many checks in small amounts.

A jobber should be chosen who carries a well-rounded stock of the types of materials most frequently ordered. Many jobbers specialize in types of books or subjects, and for fastest service these specialties should be known. A book jobber should also be located close by for obvious reasons—quicker delivery, within telephone reach at least expense, and lower transportation charges. Discounts are of least importance in choosing a jobber, since there is little or no variation among them. Many communities have local bookstores, most of which would like to sell to the surrounding libraries. Unfortunately, such an arrangement does not generally work out in practice because bookstores are not geared to jobbing, do not carry the type stock wanted, do not have good bookkeeping systems, cannot give discounts, or cannot carry unpaid accounts for any length of time.

PERIODICALS

Periodical jobbers or agents are not as numerous as book jobbers, and the library will probably have to go farther afield to find a good one. Choosing an efficient periodical agent is of prime importance, in fact, more so than for books. Periodicals can cause more trouble than any other ordering operation, and for some reason periodical publishers, on the whole, seem to be inefficient in their record keeping. It is a constant job straightening out records on subscriptions, and if an agent is not efficient, a great deal of work is involved for the acquisition librarian.

Before choosing a periodical agent, references should be obtained from other libraries in the area on the services offered by agents. An agent must be chosen who places subscriptions fast, takes care of claims rapidly, sets up accurate subscription dates, and is interested in the individual library's particular subscriptions and all the related problems.

For the serial type of government document, Bernan Associates in Washington, D. C. can make the task of subscribing to government serials a much lighter one.

OUT-OF-PRINT MATERIALS

Out-of-print dealers for both books and periodicals cannot be pinpointed as easily as in-print dealers. A good out-of-print dealer is found with experience, luck, and learning from other librarians. Usually a firm purchase order is not placed immediately with an out-of-print dealer. Quotes are requested on what is wanted, since the price is generally determined by searching charges and costs to the dealer. Dealers in this type of material advertise by mailings and through professional journals such as *Library Journal, Publishers' Weekly,* and the *Antiquarian Bookman.*

A company called University Microfilms in Ann Arbor, Michigan, specializes in making xerographic or microfilm copies of out-of-print books. The firm's *OP Catalog* lists items immediately available. It also provides copies of doctoral dissertations, early English and American books and periodicals, and modern periodicals.

FOREIGN MATERIALS

There are three principal sources for purchase of foreign materials: foreign publishers, importers of foreign materials, and foreign agents or jobbers. If there is much buying of foreign material, it is well to weigh carefully the merits of these three types of sources, keeping in mind that service is of prime importance.

Lists of foreign publishers can be found in *Europa Yearbook* and *Publishers' World*. A foreign publisher may seem the fastest, but actually he may not be. There is often a language problem, and he is apt to invoice in his local currency, making converting and paying a hardship. As with American publishers, he sells only his own publications, and he does not deal in out-of-print materials. An up-to-date list of foreign book dealers, antiquarian booksellers and publishers associations can be found in the latest *Bowker Annual*.

Gertrude Wulfekoetter states in her book on acquisition work that a library that does not do much foreign buying does well to rely on an importer in the United States who buys throughout the world, until such time as the volume of foreign purchases will warrant a library's making its own purchases abroad. One well-known importer, Stechert-Hafner International Booksellers in New York City, publishes monthly a good book selection tool called *Book News*, and any library can subscribe to this free periodical.

A United States importer will also search for out-of-print materials published in Europe. There is, of course, no language or payment problem with an importer, and he is most heavily relied upon to purchase European periodical back-sets. Periodical out-of-print importers publish catalogs of their latest back-set holdings, with prices. It is wise to acquire many of these catalogs for comparison, and it is still wiser to ask for quotations, inasmuch as the catalogs go out of date quickly.

In addition to general importers who handle books and periodicals of many countries, good service can be had from importers who specialize in a particular country or language. The British Book Center, French & European Publications, Inc., Librarie de France, and Japan Publications Trading Company, all located in New York City, show by their names their specialties. Others are given in the *Bowker Annual* buying guide.

Finally, there is the foreign agent or jobber. If there is much buying of foreign material, this writer recommends that the acquisition librarian use a foreign agent. Most foreign agents handle both new and out-of-print books. They correspond in English and invoice in American currency. It is most effective to deal with an agent in each country of origin of books purchased. The latest edition of *Clegg's International Directory of the World's Book Trade,* London, can be a useful guide in selecting agents. Recommendations of dealers whom other librarians have found satisfactory is advisable. It is no disgrace to ask questions and inquire of fellow workers their sources or procedures. A librarian is well justified in obtaining all the information he can from others who may have more experience.

BUYING

ORDER FORMS

Since bringing material into a library and through the acquisitions department is of prime importance, serious thought must be given to the mechanics of ordering. Too often libraries have very little to say about this, because ordering is done by a purchasing department on its own particular forms. However, if a purchasing department can be persuaded to let the library acquisition department place orders directly with a vendor, a far superior job will result. Fewer people will handle the ordering and receiving, and an advantage is gained in having clerks specializing in publications ordering. A clerk who orders steam rollers or microscopes cannot be expected to know also how to order a journal in French or some esoteric out-of-print title. The following paragraphs assume that the acquisitions department of a library places and receives orders. Many types of order forms are available, but only two of the most common type will be described as examples.

Many libraries use multiple order forms. These are a number of sheets of paper, usually each of a different color, fastened together for greater ease in typing, and having in between each sheet carbon or some other method of transferring type. They are usually 3 x 5 inches in size since this fits the standard-sized file drawer. Each slip has a distinct purpose and because of this, each part may differ slightly from the others. The purpose of each slip should be well thought-out before it is printed, and each should be labeled as to its use. A common set of forms contains five parts; there may be more or less depending on what is wanted from the order form. Various possible uses for the slips are the following:

> Vendor copy (the actual order)
> Library of Congress card order
> Dealer report slip
> Claim slip to dealer
> Outstanding (not yet filled) order file
> Temporary catalog card
> Invoice
> Accounting copy.

Each slip contains spaces for basic order information such as author, title, publisher, date, and price, plus spaces for additional information wanted on any individual slip. In designing multiple order forms, Gertrude Wulfekoetter gives excellent detailed information. She states succinctly, "Like so many other devices, multiple forms introduced without careful consideration of the implications of every part, and every move, can result in less, rather than more efficiency, and unit costs can be increased rather than decreased."

Some book jobbers will supply order forms, pre-addressed to themselves, free of charge. It is a good idea to arrange orders by publisher because jobbers arrange their books in this way.

Some libraries prefer using consecutively numbered order forms, usually 8½ x 11 inches in size, known as purchase orders. Many titles can be ordered on this type of form, and again they should be arranged by publisher for the jobber's convenience. If a purchase order contains many individual items, an order record giving complete information for each item must be kept separately in the outstanding order file for checking-in purposes. The most important point to remember in this arrangement is that the entry, or file-point, on the order record must correspond *exactly* to the entry on the purchase order.

When using purchase orders, one copy is sent to the vendor, one is filed alphabetically in the vendor file, and one is filed by purchase order number. A file arranged by purchase order number is important for identifying entries whose purchase order number is given on the outside of the package. (Experience has shown this writer that using titles of government documents as the main entry on order cards and purchase orders eliminates guess-work when a department, bureau, or committee is the government author.)

Material that is free should be ordered by a letter, inasmuch as a certain amount of courtesy is due the donor, and an order form is a cold business transaction. Because so much material can be obtained at no cost, it is very simple to have a form letter printed on organization letterhead.

SERIAL ORDERING

In Chapter I serials are defined as publications issued in successive parts, usually at regular intervals, and intended to be continued indefinitely. Thus, ordering serial publications to take into account this open-ended issuance schedule must be different in some ways from ordering a single book.

Since it is important that a library receive all the parts of a serial publication, a "standing order," labeled as such, is placed with a publisher or a jobber. This standing order specifies, along with the usual bibliographic information about author, title, publisher, date, and so on, with which part of the serial the library wants to begin. For example, "v. 6, 1965+" or "Part I, 1950+" means begin with volume 6, 1965 or Part I, 1950 and continue until instructed to stop. This type of order assures a library that it will automatically receive all issues of a continuing publication.

Periodicals are serial publications. Of all items that are acquired by a library, periodicals are most likely to present problems. Just as there are jobbers who specialize in books, there are jobbers, commonly called subscription agents, who specialize in periodicals. Whatever type of order

Two Sides of a Typical Periodical Record Card

PUB: Ordered from: Direct

    Bioastronautics Report
    National Press Building
    Washington 4, D. C.   Frequency: semi-monthly

No. Cop.	Requester	Date Ordered	P.O. #	Invoice Date	Cost	Subscription Dates
1	C. C. Cain	2/8/63	02434-63	3/1/63	72.00	1963 + complete back-files
1	C. C. Cain		02434-64	9/1/63	72.00	1964
2	C. C. Cain R. A. Abel		02434-65	9/6/64	72.00 ea.	1965

BIOASTRONAUTICS REPORT

3/12/63—Claimed by letter; Mr. Cain needs urgently.
4/14/63—Reply, order placed, will probably take 3-4 weeks.
      Mr. Cain notified.
5/13/63—Current issue received. Claim sent for back issues of 1963.

(Reverse Side of Periodical
Business Record)

form is used, the following information should always be included: title, length of subscription, name and address of publisher, name of vendor, person or department for whom the subscription is ordered, number of copies, cost, date subscription placed, and any billing information such as invoice number. It is important that this information be at hand for the person ordering periodicals since there are continuing transactions throughout the year on hundreds of subscription titles. Periodicals should be entered with an agent or publisher to expire at a common expiration date. Usually this is in December, since most periodicals run on a calendar year basis. Although checking a large annual renewal list is time-consuming, it is considerably less work than keeping track of subscriptions expiring at different times throughout the year.

One more point should be made about a periodical order file. It should be kept alphabetically by title and, if possible, in a visible file for ease of use. Near by, if not with the orders, should be a record of correspondence, telephone calls, telegrams, and other information relating to subscriptions, because this file will be referred to frequently.

BACK-FILE ORDERING

To buy back-files of journals, it is necessary to send a list of a library's "wants" out for quotation, just as when buying out-of-print books. Recent back-files may be available from publishers, but older runs of titles are normally purchased from dealers. The values of runs depend upon demand and scarcity, length of the run in time, and degree of completeness and condition. It is frequently well worth a higher price to buy a complete run of a periodical, since incomplete sets, although cheaper, may never be filled in, or the cost of a few rare individual volumes will boost the over-all cost. Good judgment and weighing of values is necessary in purchasing back-files. Names of dealers in this type of material can be found in the same sources mentioned for book dealers.

RECEIVING

It is rewarding to see library materials that have been ordered come in, for here is the proof that the acquisition procedure was followed and that it worked. In a large library the person who ordered the material does not necessarily also receive it, but ideally this should be the case. The person ordering is apt to be more alert in record-keeping, in checking to see that what is received is exactly what was ordered, and in being aware of what has *not* been received.

BOOKS

Receiving library materials and clearing orders is not the simple task that it first appears to be. Caution must be taken in comparing an order with the material received. Beginning library assistants may find the meanings of editions, copyright dates, and printing dates confusing. A new edition means that a book has been revised or changed and a new copyright date has been issued. Copyright information is found on the verso of the title page where it clearly states, as required by law, the latest copyright date. and the holder of the copyright. A statement to the effect that this is the second or third printing or that this is a new edition, *but with no new copyright date,* means that there is little or no change in the text. The book is essentially the same as the first printing or first edition.

Other variations that can occur between ordered and received material include: a paperback edition instead of a hard-bound edition, a similar but different title by the same author, the correct author and title but a different publisher, or a differently-priced edition. A quick flip through the pages of a new acquisition will sometimes turn up an imperfect copy in which pages are missing or duplicated, blank pages, poor printing, or covers attached upside-down. A jobber will be accommodating in accepting back faulty books or wrong orders. It is well to first write or telephone for permission to do so, however, since a pleasant working relationship is important between vendors and libraries. A simple act of this kind will assure a library of continuing good service from a dealer.

Once received material and its order correspond with each other, the order can be cleared by indicating the date of receipt and the price. The book is now ready for further processing—stamps of ownership, cataloging, and the like. The details of processing invoices for payment, which usually accompany material, are so varied from library to library that no attempt will be made to explain this step.

STANDING ORDERS

Standing order receipts are handled the same way as books, with one exception. Since many individual items will be coming in under one order, a 3 x 5 inch order or even a larger-sized purchase order does not lend itself easily to multiple receipt entries and other notes that will be recorded. The simplest method of maintaining a standing order receipt file is to use a form similar to the one illustrated.

This form is set up for use in a visible file, with the name of the publication on the bottom. All pertinent details about a serial publication can be recorded plainly for frequent use over a long period of time.

PERIODICALS

Receiving periodicals is much like receiving standing orders, except that there are many, many more of them. There could be 12, 52, or even 365 incoming items, depending on whether the periodical is a monthly, weekly, or daily. Since each item must be accounted for, a good check-in procedure must be established, preferably on a visible record file. Standard periodical check-in cards are printed by library supply houses and companies that make visible files. Cards are available for dailies or for monthlies, and the latter are adaptable for other publication schedules. This file should also be arranged alphabetically by title for ease of use. One more tip that may prove useful—in checking in

Typical Standing Order Record Card

ISSUE	REC'D	INV. NO.	AMOUNT	PUBLISHER
vol. I	4/23/63	2/23877	10.00	Academic Press
				111 Fifth Ave.
				New York 3, N. Y.

vol. II temporarily out of stock—due Nov. '63

ISSUE	REC'D	INV. NO.	AMOUNT	
vol. III	7/2/63	2/99044	15.00	

P.O. NUMBER: 12859
DATE: Jan. 18, 1963
JOBBER: Direct
BEGINNING WITH: vol. I
NO. OF COPIES: 2 each
FOR:
      main lib. (1 c.)
      branch (1 c.)

Claims/notes on reverse

ADVANCES IN APPLIED MECHANICS

5/2/63—Claim for vol. II from Academic.
5/13/63—Reply from pub that "we can't find order".
5/14/63—Ltr to pub sending copy of order and telling them they have already sent vol. I.
6/1/63—Ltr from pub that vol. II is t.o.s., will send as soon as possible.

(Reverse Side Standing Order Record)

periodicals, except dailies and weeklies, the *date* issues arrive should be recorded on the check-in cards. This establishes a pattern of receipt that enables a library to know when issues can be expected.

Two-part Claim Card

Front—filled out by library

Reverse of claim—addressed to vendor

CLAIM   Date 8/26/66

Reference: Our Letter/P.O. No.   12554

Dated: 6/2/66

May we have a report on the status of this order:

   2 copies of

             Becker, Joseph. INFORMATION STORAGE

             AND RETRIEVAL, 1963.

LOCKHEED MISSILES & SPACE COMPANY
Technical Information Center/Acquisitions
3251 Hanover Street
Palo Alto, California 94304

(THIS SIDE OF CARD IS FOR ADDRESS)

4¢
U.S.POSTAGE

        John Wiley & Sons, Inc.
        605 Third Avenue
        New York 17, N.Y.

Front—vendor's reply

Reverse of vendor's reply—addressed to library

Date __9/1/66_____

Your Order:
  Date: __6/2/66_____   P.O. No.: __12554_____

~~Was~~/will be shipped _two weeks_____   Via _air parcel post_

Out of stock_____Due_____

Back Ordered, will ship **when available**_____

Out of Print, order cancelled_____

Not our publication_____

Reprinting_ XXX _____ - _____ Due _9/10/66_____

Signed _A. A. Radcliff;_

John Wiley
605 Third Av.
New York, 17, N.Y,

(THIS SIDE OF CARD IS FOR ADDRESS)

4¢

U.S.POSTAGE

LOCKHEED MISSILES & SPACE COMPANY
Technical Information Center/Acquisitions
3251 Hanover Street
Palo Alto, California 94304

CLAIMING

Constant vigilance for missing items is a must for periodicals and standing orders. The claiming procedure should be done regularly. For periodicals this could be daily. As new issues come in, it should be noted if any previous issues have not been received. As soon as practicable claims (see illustration) should be sent, and a record kept of such claim notices. Fast claiming is important for periodicals because they go out of print quickly, and a library may find itself having to purchase missing issues. On standing orders, a regular but less frequent routine for claiming should be followed.

An excellent guide on handling periodicals is Andrew Osborne's book, *Serial Publications*. The chapters on checking in and claiming are especially recommended.

Interlibrary Loans

Interlibrary loans are a service between libraries and institutions rather than individuals. The policies and operating procedures for borrowing on interlibrary loan have been set down by the American Library Association in its pamphlet *General Interlibrary Loan Code,* one copy of which may be requested free from library supply houses. There is a small charge if more than one copy is wanted. Standard interlibrary loan request forms also may be purchased from library supply houses and are to be used as described in the ALA code. To be effective, this service is dependent upon the cooperation of all libraries using it.

It is advisable to telephone in advance to a nearby library to verify if a wanted book is available. Small libraries must be careful not to abuse the privilege of borrowing from larger libraries by keeping items beyond their due dates, by asking for the same items time after time, or by borrowing from the same library all the time unless some understanding or arrangement has been reached. Remember that the lending library is inconveniencing its own clientele for the sake of the borrowing library.

For locating periodicals, the *Union List of Serials* is the most comprehensive list for publications that started before January 1950. As mentioned previously, *New Serial Titles* is best for publications started since January 1950. There are also many local union lists covering libraries in confined geographical areas. An example is the *Union List of Periodicals: Science-Technology-Economics,* issued by the San Francisco Bay Region Chapter of Special Libraries Association. With copying services now so generally available, libraries usually do not borrow periodicals; instead the lending library reproduces a desired article. An important point to remember is that the person in charge of interlibrary loan must learn how to verify his requests as he does for any outgoing order. This saves the lending library the trouble of searching for misinformation.

Recommended Reading

ALFORD, H. W. A New Concept in Serial Dealers. *Library Resources and Technical Services,* vol. 7, no. 3, summer 1963, p. 259-63.

CHICOREL, M. Highlights in Acquisitions. *Library Resources and Technical Services,* vol. 8, no. 2, spring 1964, p. 112-25.

GINGOLD, Kurt. Translations for the U. S. Scientist. *Chemical and Engineering News*, vol. 42, no. 33, August 17, 1964, p. 88-96.

JACKSON, Isabel H., ed. *Acquisition of Special Materials*. San Francisco: San Francisco Bay Region Chapter, Special Libraries Association, 1966. ix, 232 p.

OSBORN, A. D. *Serial Publications: Their Place and Treatment in Libraries*. Chicago: American Library Association, 1955. 309 p.

WULFEKOETTER, Gertrude. *Acquisition Work: Processes Involved in Building Collections*. Seattle: University of Washington Press, 1961. 268 p.

Chapter III

The Organization of Library Materials

Marjorie Griffin, Library Manager

IBM Advanced Systems Development Division
Los Gatos, California

A LIBRARY IS A collection of information in different formats: books (fiction and non-fiction), serials, reports, and miscellanea. To approach these materials, it is necessary to have a record indicating what books and other materials a library possesses. It is as necessary to help borrowers locate books they can specify by author, title, or by subject as it is to assist them in finding the right books when they do not know precisely what they want. To ensure this, library materials must be organized in some predetermined scheme; this is commonly called classification.

Book Classification

Classification is an ordered arrangement in which books treating a similar subject are grouped together; those of related subjects are grouped nearby. This arrangement facilitates searching for a book, because it is easier to look in a subject area on the shelves than to hunt for a book by author or title. Browsers prefer to examine books on the shelf rather than search through cards.

A cataloger assumes the major responsibility for identifying the contents of a book. He must determine the intent of the author, the topics of interest, and select the terms to express the content of the book, briefly and precisely. A cataloger must think in terms of serving the special subject interests of library users, especially when considering a book whose contents can be placed in more than one category, i.e., he must decide which classification will be most useful. To identify a book in its correct area on the shelf and to make its classification significant, a notation scheme is used. This lettering or numbering, printed on the spine of the book, specifies both its proper location on the shelf and its contents.

To develop consistency in arrangements, classification schemes that divide knowledge into classes, with allied subjects as divisions and subdivisions, have been prepared. The two major schemes are the Library of Congress system, developed for that institution, and the Dewey Decimal Classification. In the former, there are 21 major class areas with sub-classes. The Dewey Decimal is divided into ten major groups of knowledge, sub-divided by decimals. The Library of Congress publishes a separate schedule for each class. In the Dewey Decimal scheme (17th edition, volume 2), an index follows the classification schedule. When the broad subject of a book has been determined, the cataloger checks in this index to pinpoint the contents; the contents then will direct him to a call number. The Library of Congress classification, being more definitive and expressive, is used largely in university and research libraries and special libraries. The Dewey Decimal is easier to remember and has been applied most frequently in public and school libraries.

Examples of Classification Sub-divisions

LIBRARY OF CONGRESS CLASSIFICATION		DEWEY DECIMAL CLASSIFICATION	
T	Technology	600	Applied Science
TA	Engineering—General	610	Medicine
TC	Hydraulic Engineering	620	Engineering
TD	Municipal Engineering	630	Agriculture
TE	Roads and Pavements	640	Home Economics
TF	Railroad Engineering	650	Communication and Business
TG	Bridge Engineering	660	Chemical Technology
TH	Building	670	Manufactures
TJ	Mechanical Engineering	680	Mechanic Trades
TK	Electrical Engineering	690	Building

Further Breakdown of Library of Congress Classification

TJ   **TJ**

MECHANICAL ENGINEERING AND MACHINERY

175	**Principles of mechanism. Kinematics of machinery. Mechanical movements.**
181	General.
	Special movements and devices.
.5	The wheel.
	Belt-gearing, Belts, Pulleys, etc., *see* TJ 1100-1119.
182	Links and link-motion. Cranks.
183	Hooke's and other link-couplings.
	Toothed gears. Gearing.
184	General.
185	Tables, lists, etc.
186	Laying out gear-teeth. Odontographs.
187	Gear-cutting machines.
188	Catalogs.

Further Breakdown of the Dewey Decimal Classification

621.79	Other shops and departments
.8	**Principles of mechanism Power transmission Hoisting and conveying machinery**
.81	General Principles of mechanism Machine design
.82	Journals, shafting, etc.
.821	Journals
.822	Bearings: ball, roller, etc. Hangers Bearing metals
.823	**Shafting**
.8235	Flexible shafting
.825	Couplings and clutches Universal joints
	Friction clutches
.826	Shaft brakes
.83	Tooth gears and cams

Special classifications have been written for libraries that specialize in a single subject. For example, the Harvard Business Library is noted for its scheme outlining business literature—*A Classification of Business Literature* (Library of Harvard University Graduate School of Business Administration. New York: Shoe String Press, Inc. 1960). In this scheme, letters of the alphabet define the major subjects (see illustration). Other libraries have modified this scheme by adding different letters to indicate sub-divisions, creating the typical hierarchy in which one works from the general to the specfic in a classification scheme.

A Section of the Harvard Business Library Classification

The main stem of the classification, that relating to business and allied fields, contains the following main sections:

- A. Business: Generalia and general relations to government
- B. Business and economic theory
- C. Social theories and problems
- D. Methodology of research and control
- E. Economic resources
- F. Business and economic conditions
- G. Business and economic history
- H. Business organization and administration
- I. Industrial management
- J. Money, banking and finance
- K. Financial institutions
- L. Insurance
- M. Land and land economics
- N. Labor and labor organization
- Q. Primary industries and engineering
- R. Manufacturing industries. Construction. Services
- S. Marketing
- T. Foreign marketing
- V-Y. Public utilities: transportation, communication, etc.

Use of Subject, Industries, and Local Lists in Combination.

If it is decided to divide the material on a certain subject by the industries to which it relates, the numerals of the Industries List may be appended to the appropriate letter notation. Such numerals would be separated from the letters of the chief notation by a colon (:). The following are examples of this combination:

BUSINESS

ASJN	Transportation and communication
ASJP	Admission and dues
ASJS	Stocks. Bonds. Rights
ASJT	Movement of goods
	Import duties. See AU, TH
	Export duties. See AUAK, TAU
ASJW	Transit duties
ASJX	Octrol
ASK	Franchises. Licenses
	Payments made for the privilege of carrying on business or engaging in a profession or occupation
	For public utility franchises see Franchises under V, W or Y
ASKL	Fees
	Payments made for recording, registration, inspection and like governmental services
ASL	Exemption
	If preferred, exemption of a particular form of tax may be classified with that tax, i.e. Public property. See ASD
ASM	Incidence. Tax shifting (theory)
ASMV	Evasion
ASN	Situs of taxpayer (individual or corporation)
ASNJ	Foreign, alien (non-resident of state, extra-state)
ASNL	Domestic, citizen (resident of state, intra-state)
ASO	Situs of taxables
	Includes double taxation
ASOH	Property
ASOF	Inheritance
ASOH	Income

Additional examples of special classification schemes may be found at the Bibliographic Systems Center, located at the School of Library Science, Western Reserve University in Cleveland, Ohio. The Center is a lending service charged with acquiring, maintaining, and organizing a definitive collection of classifications other than the popular Library of Congress or the Dewey Decimal systems. In addition the Center maintains files of subject heading lists, thesauri, terminology lists, dictionaries, and works about classification and subject headings, discussed in more detail below.

Another tool that can help assure consistency and uniform practice in assigning class numbers is the shelf list. This is a guide to material already processed in the library, arranged in the same order in which books are found on the shelf, i.e., by classification number. The same subject heading should always be used for books with similar contents, and they should be placed near one another on the shelf.

Subject Headings

Subject headings express the contents of a book in established terms that a borrower can recognize. A cataloger may use as many subject headings as necessary to describe a book; they supplement the title and make classification more specific. Accuracy in choosing subject headings is essential for the effective use of books. For a direct approach, specific headings are preferable to general ones.

Cross references indicate other material on related subjects and may be "see" and "see also" references. A "see" reference directs a borrower to the subject heading used by a library; a "see also" reference indicates that there is more information found under the headings suggested. As a guide and to preserve continuity in assigning subjects, an authority list is kept, with each subject on a separate card and the cards arranged in alphabetical order. Consistency in selecting subject headings is achieved

Library of Congress List of Subject Headings

Mechanical draft. *(TJ335)*
   x Draft, Mechanical.
     Draught, Mechanical.
Mechanical drawing. *(T351-377)*
   sa Architectural drawing.
     Design, Industrial.
     Drawing-room practice.
     Geometrical drawing.
     Graphic methods.
     Graphic statics.
     Isometric projection.
     Machinery—Drawing.
     Projection.
     Structural drawing.
     Tinting.
   x Drafting, Mechanical.
     Engineering drawing.
     Industrial drawing.
     Mathematical drawing.
     Plans
     Technical drawing.
  xx Design, Industrial.
     Drawing.
     Drawing instruments.
     Engineering.
     Geometrical drawing.

by referring to the authority list, the shelf list, and to general aids such as the following books.

Library of Congress List of Subject Headings is particularly important with the LC classification system, since it gives the LC notation. In the examples on page 38 note the *sa* directs one to more specific headings. The *x* indicates "refer from (see); do not use this heading," the *xx* indicates "refer from (see also)."

Sears' List of Subject Headings for Small Libraries is for public and school libraries where subjects are more general. This book gives the Dewey Decimal number recommended for each subject.

Subject Collections, compiled by Lee Ash, is arranged in broad subject areas and lists libraries using special classifications, e.g., under Mechanical Engineering there are listed the libraries of the U. S. Department of the Navy, Caterpillar Tractor Company, and Indiana Technical College Library.

Indexes provide good sources of information for delimiting specific entries where subjects are nearly alike. The necessary distinctions cannot always be made solely on the basis of predetermined subject lists, which cannot be updated often enough to include narrow breakdowns in special subjects. Helpful indexes include *Art Index, Biological Abstracts, Business Periodicals Index, Chemical Abstracts, Engineering Index, Public Affairs Information Service, Index Medicus,* and *Readers' Guide to Periodical Literature.*

Book Cataloging

Transferring information about a book to a card according to set rules is known as cataloging. The prepared catalog cards are arranged alphabetically in trays (drawers) to comprise the card catalog. This catalog provides a three-way approach to information—by author, title, and subject. The card catalog thus interprets a library to a reader: *1)* by recording the books in the library by author and by title, *2)* by indicating the subject contents of the books, and *3)* by bringing the needs of the user and the resources of the library together.

A card catalog can be divided in three different ways: *1)* as a *dictionary catalog,* in which all cards have been arranged in alphabetical order, *2)* as a *divided catalog,* in which all subject cards are filed in one catalog and all author, title, and added entry cards are filed in another, and *3)* as a *classified catalog,* in which cards are arranged by their classification number just as books are placed on the shelves.

Types of Cards

The AUTHOR CARD (also called the main entry, unit card, or official entry) is the basic card and contains the complete information, i.e., call number, author heading, title of book, imprint, collation, notes, and tracing.

The ADDED ENTRY is a duplicate of the author card with the addition

Set of Author(s), Title, and Subject Cards for One Book

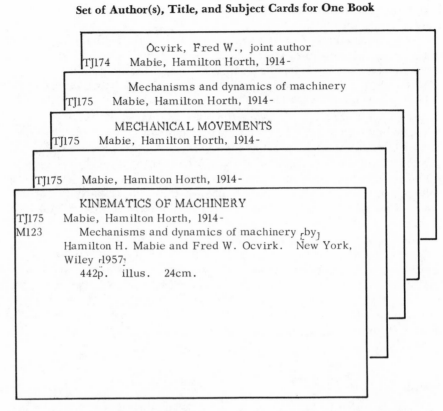

of a special heading indented above the author on the top line of the card. These cards are typed or printed according to a pattern.

The designation of joint author, editor, compiler, or translator is indicated after the name by an abbreviation, i.e., jt. auth., ed., comp., tr.

SUBJECT CARDS have the subject (content) of the book printed in red or in capital letters at the top of the card to distinguish them from the author or title cards.

TITLE CARDS have the title repeated on the top line.

ANALYTIC CARDS identify small units of information such as chapters within a book, plays or poems within a collection, or short stories.

CROSS REFERENCE CARDS refer a borrower to other places to look in the catalog. A "see" card indicates there is no information under this subject heading but refers the user to other headings. The "see also" card refers the reader to additional material that is closely related but filed under a different heading.

COMPONENTS OF CATALOG CARD

A standard 3 x 5 catalog card is developed in the following pattern. This format can vary slightly with each library.

The CALL NUMBER is composed of two elements, the subject classification of the book, and the author number. In the illustration "TJ175" represents the subject as shown in the tracings, the "M" is the initial letter of the author's last name, and the "123" places the author alphabetically within all other authors whose name begins with "M" within that classification number.

The AUTHOR'S NAME is typed approximately 8 spaces from the left edge of the card to make it conspicuous. This may be a personal name or a corporate name, and its position is commonly called the first indention.

The TITLE OF THE BOOK is typed at the second indention (approximately 12 spaces), starting underneath the fifth letter of the author's name. The card thus assumes the appearance of a paragraph, because the second line of the title starts under the third letter of the author's name.

The IMPRINT, comprising the place of publication, publisher's name, and date of publication usually follows the title after a gap of 3 spaces to distinguish it from other information. Where more than one city is mentioned, the first city will be the home office. Frequently the date will be found on the reverse of the title page. Use the latest copyright date.

The COLLATION, indicating volumes, pages, illustrations, plates, maps,

Cross Reference Cards

Kinetics

see

Dynamics

Mechanical movements

see also

Machinery, Kinematics of

Parts of a Library of Congress Card

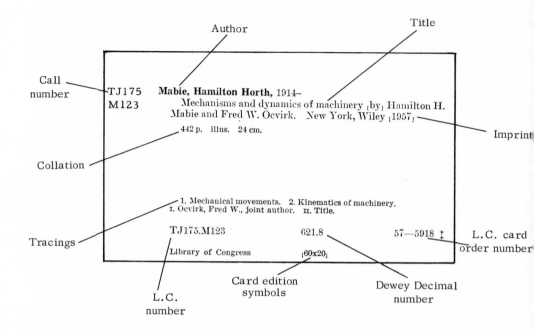

and references, is typed at the second indention, on the line below the imprint.

NOTES, indicating contents, series, or special bibliographic information, are printed below the collation at the second indention.

TRACINGS, the record of all cards made for one book, are most frequently located on the back of the shelf list card, typed upside down for convenience, or on the author card. These indicate to a typist the added cards, and if a book is discarded or lost, will indicate which cards to withdraw from the catalog. On the printed cards available from the Library of Congress, the tracings are found on the front of the card, below the notes.

A printed LC card contains this additional information: the LC CLASSIFICATION NUMBER, assigned by the Library of Congress, the DEWEY DECIMAL NUMBER, assigned by the Library of Congress for catalogers who use that system, the LC ORDER NUMBER, which is required when one orders LC cards, and the CARD SYMBOL, a notation in the center of the LC card that signifies the edition and the number of cards printed.

The Wilson catalog card published by the H. W. Wilson Company is a simple entry with an annotation of the book. These can be purchased with or without subject headings that conform to the Sears Subject Heading List.

```
TJ175    Mabie, Hamilton Horth, 1914-
M123         Mechanisms and dynamics of machinery ₍by₎
         Hamilton H. Mabie and Fred W. Ocvirk.   New York,
         Wiley ₍1957₎

4372     8-4-61    c.1    Stacey's      $8.50
5212     7-7-62    c.2    Gift          gratis
```

Shelf List Card

The shelf list card duplicates the main entry card but omits the notes and contents. This card must include all accession numbers for each title, source data, and cost of each book. Shelf list cards are usually kept in the work area of the library for frequent checking by catalogers. The cards are arranged in call number order exactly as the books are arranged on the shelf. The reasons for keeping a shelf list file are: 1) to avoid duplication in ordering books, 2) to insure uniformity in classifying, 3) to assist with inventory, 4) to show how many books are in one class or in the library (for statistics), 5) to assist a cataloger to avoid duplicating numbers when classifying, and 6) to present in one location a record of the number of copies of a title in the collection.

Book Labeling and Book Pockets

Book labeling is accomplished by marking a book spine with straight plain lettering and figures that identify it on a shelf by its call number. Labeling helps a borrower locate a book, and helps a library assistant to return each book to its proper place. The correct call number should appear on the spine of the book, on the book pocket, and on the circulation card. For the sake of shelf appearance, labeling on the spine should begin at the same distance from the bottom of all books.

The book pocket holds the circulation card when the book is on the shelf; it may be placed inside either the front or back cover. The call number, author, title, and copy or accession number are typed on book pockets so that assistants can identify accurately and easily the correct

Book Pocket and Book Labeling

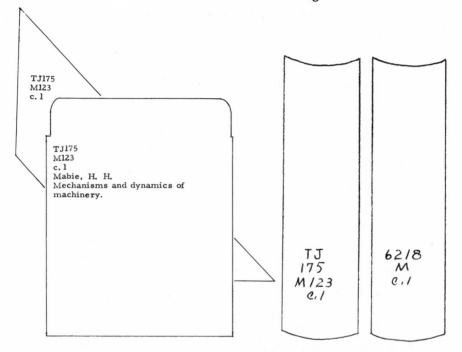

book card to place in the pocket before the book is returned to the shelf. If he places the incorrect book card inside, a problem is created for two borrowers.

Arrangement of Cards in Catalog

Cards must be arranged so that those with the same subject headings will be filed together, and cards with unlike entries also be filed in some definite order. The rules for grouping cards are given below.

Guide cards should be prepared to indicate approximate location of cards, and may follow either of two standard practices: *1)* in a dictionary catalog, surnames will be on the left, main subject headings in the center, and the subdivision of a subject on the right (see illustration), and *2)* where preferred, a straight alphabetical breakdown may be used, with a guide card every two inches.

To allow for expansion, it is advisable to fill file drawers no more than two-thirds full. Drawers are labeled so that a user can find information by author, title, or subject.

There are different rules for filing cards. It is not important which method has been adopted by the library, but it is important that there be uniformity in practice so that a borrower, once he understands the particular system, can expect consistency.

Guide Card Arrangement in a Dictionary Catalog

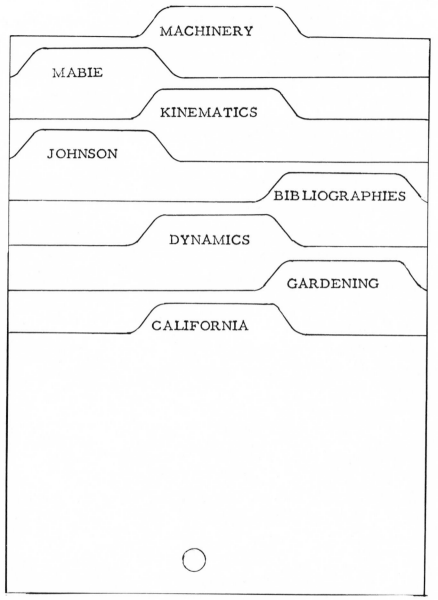

WORD-BY-WORD FILING

The basic rule according to American Library Association standards is to arrange each entry in alphabetical order to the end of each word, ignoring initial articles in the title. This method of filing is frequently called "nothing before something." For example:

> Book
> Book Collecting
> Book of English Essays
> Bookbinding

LETTER-BY-LETTER FILING

In this alternate method, spaces between words are not considered. For example:

> Book
> Bookbinding
> Book Collecting
> Book of English Essays

DICTIONARY CATALOG FILING

When entries begin with the same word in a dictionary catalog, the order recommended by ALA is *person, place, subject,* and *title.* For example:

> London, George
> London, Eng.
> LONDON, ENG.
> London Old and New

Other Rules

Abbreviations are arranged as though spelled in full except for Mr. and Mrs., for example:

> St. Denis, Ruth
> Saint-Exupery
> St. Joan
> Saint Lawrence River

Works *by* an author precede works *about* an author.

A subdivision of a subject is separated from the main subject by a hyphen; where a subject heading is followed by a descriptive adjective, they are separated by a comma. There are two acceptable ways of filing: *1)* keep hyphenated subdivisions together, for example:

> Education
> Education-Bibliography
> Education-History
> Education, Comparative

or, *2)* disregard all punctuation, for example:

> Education
> Education-Bibliography
> Education, Comparative
> Education-History

It should be stressed that uniformity in practice is more important in a library than the particular method of filing chosen. Library borrowers can adapt to any system, providing there is consistency.

Serials

Serials are publications issued in successive parts and intended to be continued indefinitely.

PERIODICALS

Periodicals form a valuable part of a library collection and need to be processed for the following reasons: *1)* they publish immediate results of experiments in research and announce technical developments, *2)* they represent a continuous record of scientific advance; therefore, they increase in value, and *3)* back-files of periodicals include processes and techniques that are seldom published in books; therefore, they are more valuable than books in some libraries.

Arrangement

The arrangement of periodicals varies in different libraries, depending upon the significance of periodicals in the collection. Some libraries catalog periodicals so that books and periodicals of similar subjects will be together.

As there is no author, and the editor will change, the main entry of a periodical is the title. This title entry is distinguished from the conventional title entry by being typed as a *hanging indention*. This means in-

Periodical Catalog Card

The **Physical** review; a journal of **experimental and theoreti-**
cal physics. v. 1–35, July 1893–Dec. 1912; ser. 2, v. 1–
Jan. 1913–
₁Lancaster, Pa., etc.₁ Published for the American Physical
Society by the American Institute of Physics ₁etc.₁

   v. in   illus. 25–28 cm.

   Bimonthly, July 1893–June 1897; monthly (irregular) July 1897–
June 1929; semimonthly, July 1929–
   Ser. 2, v. 41–60 (July 1932–Dec. 1941) issued without subtitle.
   Published for Cornell University, July 1893–Jan. 1903.
   "Conducted with the co-operation of the American Physical Society,"
Feb. 1903–Dec. 1912.

                        (Continued on next card)
                                          12—37719*
                        ₁56r53e2₁

47

denting every line down to the collation instead of typing them in paragraph form. Volumes are labeled with a call number and shelved with the books.

Some libraries shelve periodicals by issuing society so that all publications will be together, for example:

American Mathematical Society.   Bulletin
                                 Notices
                                 Transactions

Other libraries prefer to shelve strictly by title because the librarians consider that borrowers recall periodicals by their title, for example:

Bulletin of the American Mathematical Society
Notices of the American Mathematical Society
Transactions of the American Mathematical Society

BINDING PERIODICALS

Decisions about binding periodicals or monographs are based on their value to an organization. Those searched frequently for articles are of permanent value and should be bound. When binding is found advisable, it is essential, for ready reference, that all issues constituting a volume be bound with the index or table of contents and the title page. It is customary for the table of contents to be bound in the front, while the index is bound in the back. Each volume is bound as a unit unless: 1) so few issues comprise a volume that two volumes can be bound together for economy. (In such a case, the volumes are separated by the index for the first volume and by a colored page inserted as a divider.) or, 2) if a single volume is too thick (over three inches), it is divided and bound in two parts. The part containing the index will be so labeled on the spine.

A binding record should be kept with other records for each serial, e.g., with the check-in card maintained for each periodical received. Complete instructions should be attached to volumes sent to the bindery. These instructions must include the title, volume, year, inclusive paging if a separated volume, color of binding, and also show the regular spacing desired. Some binderies require the latter information only on the first volume to be bound, since they make a rubbing that is kept on file for future volumes of each title. Volumes returned from the bindery must be checked to make sure that the information printed on the spine corresponds to the contents of the volume and to be certain that the inner margin is generous enough to allow for reproducing complete pages with equipment that requires the book to be spread open.

Patterns of usage and the frequency of a periodical will influence the choice of binding for serials of temporary value. Some libraries place these in pamphlet boxes or between stiff covers tied with a cord at the margin; still others use liquid plastic for binding. The advantages of binding are that: 1) individual issues cannot be lost, 2) bound volumes are easier to refer to and to handle, 3) individual volumes are easier to

Examples of Titles as Main Entries

```
310          The world almanac and book of facts. . .
N            New York World-Telegram


             Library has:
             1960
             1961
             1962
```

```
030          Encyclopaedia Britannica; a new survey of
E            universal knowledge.   14th ed.
             Encyclopaedia Britannica, 1952.
             24v.   illus.   maps.   ports.
```

find when many volumes of a periodical are shelved together, and *4)* bound periodicals use less space than unbound ones.

ANNUAL REPORTS, DIRECTORIES, MONOGRAPHS, and YEARBOOKS

These are publications listed in successive parts, including such yearbooks as the *World Almanac and Book of Facts,* that are found in most libraries. Since there is no author, and since editors of such publications change, the main entry card is again the title with a hanging indention. This card must show which issues of each publication the library holds; this is indicated as a note at the second indention after "Library has." It is equally important to show the frequency of issue on the card, i.e., annual or biennial.

Technical Reports

Technical reports constitute, in some technical libraries, the most vital part of the collection. The information they contain is more current than that in periodicals or books, because reports must be written on the progress of many technical projects at specified intervals. Frequently these reports contain information that is never published in any other form; and as unique records of original work, they must be located easily and quickly. Libraries usually maintain files of both internal reports (written within an organization) and external reports (received from other companies doing comparable work).

In discussing technical report literature several new forms of library jargon must be introduced. Because of the rapid growth of the number of technical reports, there has been a strong movement toward storing and retrieving this type of material by the use of data-processing equipment. Such words as computers, magnetic tape, punched cards, key-punching, and card sorters are introduced frequently when considering the organization of technical report literature. The new terminology resulting from this relationship between the data-processing field and technical reports need not be confusing. Terms such as indexing, thesaurus, Uniterm, permuted titles, have their counterparts in common library language.

Indexing technical reports means cataloging them. Part of the cataloging process for books discussed earlier in this chapter was the assignment of subjects, usually taken from lists of subject headings. When an indexer (instead of cataloger) indexes a technical report, he chooses descriptors (instead of subjects) by referring to a thesaurus (instead of a subject heading list). The end result of indexing a technical report is usually a card similar to a conventional card catalog, but there are other methods of listing holdings of library materials, two of which are described in the section below.

IDENTIFICATION AND INDEXING

To enable anyone to approach technical reports, it is mandatory that each be meticulously documented by corporate entry (originating organization), author, title, report number, project number, contract number, date, and subject. There are several methods of indexing the contents of reports.

Uniterm Indexing

A Uniterm (made up of the words "unit" and "term") method consists of single words or combinations of words standing for single concepts, e.g., human engineering, to designate the subject content of documents. Note that Uniterms are concepts, not subject headings. Usually each term is listed as a heading on a separate card, with the library identification number of the documents containing this descriptor entered in columns below. A user wanting information on "strain gauges" would select the cards headed by "Strain" and by "Gauge." Then he would match identical numbers on each card. The reports with these matching numbers would be pulled from the files as being on the subject of strain gauges.

Uniterm Cards for "Strain" and "Gauge." The Circled Numbers Show Reports about "Strain Gauges."

STRAIN									
381 111 151	102 (492) 552 682	123 333 383	124 (154)	295 (305) 315	206 396 426 476	(417)	128 158	229 319 460	110 150

GAUGE									
211	142 (492) 512	133 173	(154) 184 394	175 285 (305) 325	196 276	287 307 (417)	198 228	219	120 160 270 340

THESAURI

Some libraries give each report subject headings from a published thesaurus such as one of these:

DDC (The Defense Documentation Center) *Thesaurus of Descriptors*
Nuclear Science Abstracts

Engineering Index
Science Abstracts
Chemical Engineering Thesaurus
Chemical Abstracts
Engineers Joint Council Thesaurus of Engineering Terms

KWIC INDEXING

KWIC (Keyword in Context) indexing is a listing of significant words in the title of a document that is permuted so that each word is in alphabetical order in a column along with the partial or whole title to show context. This refers users to a code number to locate the report. Each document appears in a KWIC index as many times as there are significant words in the title. To permute a title means simply "to change the order or arrangement of." For example, the title of this book, *The Library: An Introduction for Library Assistants,* filed under L, can be permuted to *Introduction for Library Assistants, The Library:,* filed under I, or *Library Assistants, The Library: An Introduction for,* filed under L, or *Assistants, The Library: An Introduction for Library,* filed under A. The permuted title method provides a fast subject or concept approach to the literature so indexed.

OTHER SYSTEMS

An author index makes it possible to determine what has been written by a certain man. If he has not published any articles or books, the author report file may be the only source of information.

Some technical reports are distributed with catalog cards in the back of the report. It is more frequent now, however, to find a form listing all the necessary biblographic information, plus key words pertaining to the report. This is extremely useful in indexing and provides uniformity of main entry and other details.

Report catalog cards have a different format from those for books or periodicals. Usually the title is predominant to assist a user in identifying the material. Sometimes abstracts of the contents are included on the card.

FILING

Reports must be filed as accurately as they are cataloged, and each entry in the catalog should be thoroughly cross-referenced to lead a user to the correct document. Reports can be filed alphabetically by the issuing agency (corporate author) and then numerically by report number or by date. Some libraries prefer to give each report an accession number and file by this, totally disregarding any grouping by source. Still other libraries will file reports by personal or corporate author and others in broad subject groupings. Each method has advantages and disadvantages depending upon library usage, but ease of retrieval is the most important consideration. No method will be good if the established pattern is not followed consistently and if the cross-references are not sufficient to identify the report by its various entries.

SECURITY-CLASSIFIED REPORTS

Company or government reports that contain classified information are specially classified for national security reasons. If a report contains company trade information (termed "company confidential"), these reports remain within the company to ensure that the information they contain does not reach competitors; if reports are government reports, i.e., if the research was paid for with public funds, they will be restricted for use by other contractors with security clearances. These strict measures are taken to safeguard information deemed vital to national defense. Security-classified documents must be handled according to rigid regulations, and librarians responsible for them must have security clearances themselves.

Miscellaneous Materials

Special libraries, in particular, have many types of material peculiar to the special interests of the organizations they serve. Public libraries, too, may have collections of clippings, maps, and miscellaneous documents. It is essential that such items be recorded and identified distinctly so that they can be retrieved as needed.

PATENTS

Patents are single documents representing an agreement between a government and an inventor. They should be indexed minutely and identified by patentee, assignee, subject, and number. There should be separate approaches to all this information in a card catalog. United States patents are filed by the Patent Office classification scheme; foreign patents by country and then by number. The means of approaching the ordered arrangement, either on the shelf or in filing cabinets, is through the card catalog.

CLIPPINGS

Clippings keep up with the most current information on selected subjects. They are used extensively in newspaper and publishing house libraries. Each must be identified immediately by source—the newspaper name and date or periodical title, volume, date, and pages. Clippings are most often filed in envelopes under broad subject headings arranged in alphabetical order, frequently after they have been routed to personnel interested in the subject. The subject headings are of considerable importance, since they are usually the only method by which clippings are arranged and retrieved. If a clipping covers more than one subject, either a copy or a reference to it should be located under the secondary subject.

GOVERNMENT DOCUMENTS

Government documents are treated as individual pamphlets if only a few are received in the library; they are filed all together if many are received. If documents belong to a series, they should be arranged as a series of bulletins or technical papers according to a serial number. If documents are not part of a series, it is easiest to file them alphabetically by issuing agency and then in numerical sequence. Government documents as considered here are those found in the *Monthly Catalog,* i.e. Congressional proceedings, department reports, hearings, and all manner of public information widely available.

PAMPHLETS

Pamphlets are publications, generally of temporary value and usually 64 pages or less, that are more conveniently kept in a vertical file than on a shelf. They may be filed by author or issuing agent with no further indexing, or arranged systematically by subject. Cross references must be used to help users who may recall and identify a pamphlet in a variety of ways. Indexing schemes will range from simple, broad subject categories to the minutely detailed, depending upon the volume of this material and its usage in different libraries. Some libraries distinguish pamphlets by colored cards in the card catalog and mark both the cards and pamphlets with a simple notation. Ideally, libraries should weed their collections annually or biannually.

PICTURES

Pictures are an important part of the collections in museum, art, motion picture and advertising libraries. To serve their purpose, they must be identified accurately and completely as to subject, format, and source. Subject headings may be broad or specific depending on the range of usage in the library. Subject headings are sometimes taken from *Readers' Guide, PAIS* (Public Affairs Information Service) or the *Vertical File Service.*

Negatives require special care if they are to remain useful. They should be kept in clear plastic covers or envelopes for protection against abrasion and handling.

MAPS

Maps are important to petroleum, geological, highway engineering, and other library collections. Again, detailed indexing and identification as to source and type are essential for locating information. Entry to maps is by a classification scheme or index, depending upon what will be most useful in the particular library. The entry should state whether a map is physical, political, or geographical, its scale, authority, and projection, and the date of printing (so that users are not misled by obsolete material). Maps should be arranged geographically by country, state, type, and quadrangle name.

TRADE LITERATURE

Information in this category will range from price lists to minute specifications of components. The approaches to the information will be by manufacturer's name, by trade name, and by product. *Thomas' Register of American Manufacturers* is one excellent published guide to such information; *Chemical Week Buyers' Guide* and *Electronics Buyers' Guide* are others.

MICROFORMS

Microforms are usually of three types: microfilm, microfiche, and Microcards. Microfilm is the most familiar, being most often the 35mm size, with each frame containing at least one page of the material. Microfiche is becoming more widely known because of its adoption as a standard form by several federal agencies. "Fiche" is a French term meaning "filing-card," the most common size being 4 x 6 inches and containing up to 60 or more pages of material. The Microcard is not film but rather an opaque positive print made from a negative microfiche. Microcards are usually 3 x 5 inches, each with about 40 pages of text.

Each form has its advantages and disadvantages, although microfiche seems to have the most advantages in handling, storing, cost, and use. All the microforms, of course, require a mechanical reader of some type, and hard-copy full-sized pages can be produced directly from microfilm and -fiche, while no copies can be made directly from Microcards. Each of the forms usually has an eye-legible heading containing the appropriate bibliographic information. Accurate labeling is essential for effective use of this material.

In organizing a collection of microforms, it is necessary to be guided by frequency of use. Information in a card catalog must stipulate details of the size of film, microform used, length of roll of film or number of Microcards or -fiche, and whether positive or negative, in addition to the basic entry of author, issuing agency, title, date, and subject. Most frequently, microfilm is kept in numeric sequence with entry from author, title, issuing agency, and subject. Microfilm on reels must be kept in suitable cabinets, while microfiche and Microcards can be filed in standard card-sized drawers.

SLIDES, PHONOGRAPH RECORDS, AND TAPES

Slides, phonograph records, and tapes require meticulous indexing because it is difficult or impossible to refer to the actual source material. A library should try to make the catalog of this type of material as detailed and as explicit as possible to assure efficient retrieval.

Recommended Reading

AKERS, Susan Grey. *Simple Library Cataloguing.* Chicago: American Library Association, 1944. 197 p.

BROWN, M. C. In-Service Training and Decision-Making in the Catalog Department. *Library Resources and Technical Services,* vol. 5, no. 1, Winter 1961, p. 82-6.

DAVINSON, D. E. *Periodicals, a Manual of Practice for Librarians.* London: Grafton & Co., 1960. 165 p.

FRY, Bernard M. *Library Organization and Management of Technical Reports Literature*. Washington, D. C.: Catholic University of America Press, 1953. 140 p.

JOLLEY, L. *The Principles of Cataloguing*. London: Crosby Lockwood & Son, 1960. 147 p.

JOYCE, C. Cataloging by and for Amateurs. *Library Journal*, vol. 86, no. 3, February 15, 1961, p. 743-6.

KAISER, W. H. Synchronized Book Processing. *Library Journal*, vol. 86, no. 3, February 15, 1961, p. 752-4.

KEEFER, M. Simplified Cataloguing of Federal and State Documents. *Library Resources and Technical Services*, vol. 6, no. 3, Summer 1962, p. 262-4.

LYNDENBERG, Harry Miller, and ARCHER, John. *The Care and Repair of Books*, 4th ed., rev. by John Alden. New York: R. R. Bowker, 1960. 122 p.

MANN, Margaret. *Introduction to Cataloguing and the Classification of Books*, 2nd ed. Chicago: American Library Association, 1946. 276 p.

PIERCY, Esther J. *Commonsense Cataloging: A Manual for the Organization of Books and Other Materials in School and Small Public Libraries*. New York: H. W. Wilson, 1965. 223 p.

VICKERY, B. C. *Classification and Indexing in Science*. New York: Academic Press, 1958. 185 p.

WEEKS, Bertha M. *Filing and Records Management*, 3rd rev. ed. New York: Ronald, 1964. 287 p.

Chapter IV

Library Services

Based on a paper by
Robert S. Meyer, Head Librarian

Lawrence Radiation Laboratory
University of California
Berkeley, California

THE THINGS learned so far—the introduction to libraries and the practices of acquisitions, cataloging, and processing of material —are all necessary parts of the picture. Now that picture must be completed by asking, "What has this all been for, why have these things been done, what happens to these processed materials?" The answer is in the services that are given to a library's users.

Circulation

The major purpose of circulation procedures is to have a record of items charged out of the library. This protects library property and enables a library to know the location of items not found on the shelves. The detailed steps of acquisition and cataloging mean nothing if the material a catalog card represents is not in its proper place. The service a library can render suffers if there is no adequate circulation routine.

A vital point to keep in mind here, as in all other library matters, is the maintenance of good will and satisfaction of borrowers. It must always be remembered that library rules, procedures, and even the collection itself, are only means to an end and not ends in themselves. A library collection is for use; it is not just to be stored. Therefore, circulation regulations should be as permissive as possible, with restrictions introduced only when the convenience of one borrower might cause greater inconvenience to other borrowers. The more attention paid to the needs, habits, and desires of the users, the better the service rendered.

A library assistant plays an important role in circulation work in representing the library to a reader. In charging materials out, in locating materials, and in explaining the rules and procedures to users, it is essential that circulation personnel project a friendly and helpful image of the library that will encourage a user to return and to continue to use its services. The voice on the telephone, the manner at the desk, even the writing on the overdue notices, are all major points of contact between a library and its clientele.

BASIC TYPES OF CIRCULATION SYSTEMS

Although a 1961 study revealed about 28 major circulation systems in use by libraries, most are variations of two basic types, the Newark system and the transaction system.

The Newark system was developed around the turn of the century and is used by most special libraries. It is extremely simple, requiring only that a book card or charge slip be filled out for each item being borrowed and that this record be kept in an orderly arrangement until the item is returned. An important feature of this system, in addition to its simplicity, is that information concerning the location of every item is always readily available.

The transaction system is used by many public libraries to reduce the amount of work required to keep circulation records for large or heavily-used collections. The principle is that since most items are returned on time or shortly thereafter, great effort is saved if records are kept for just the relatively few items that become overdue. This seemingly impossible task is accomplished by first photographing onto a reel of film pertinent details about the book and the borrower, combined with a serially-numbered transaction card. The transaction card is put into the book pocket when the book is charged out and is removed and filed back into numerical order when the book is returned. By checking this file at appropriate intervals, one can easily note which transaction cards are missing. Then by checking the film, an unreturned book and its borrower can be identified. This system is quite rapid in use but has the weakness of not providing information about books in circulation, because the arrangement of the filmed charges is not one that can easily be consulted as it is in purely chronological order.

This difference between the two major types of circulation systems illustrates something that must frequently be pointed out—there usually isn't any one right answer to most library procedures. The differences among procedures are often due, as they should be, to the differences in types of libraries and their objectives, users, and collections. It is most rewarding to try to identify the factors that account for one library's operations being similar to some others, different from still others, and perhaps unique in some ways. The more a library can tailor-make its operations to suit its own individual environment, the more successful it will be.

At present, manual circulation systems are more widely used than are mechanical systems. Generally, manual systems are more satisfactory for most libraries because they are more economical, more flexible, and require less maintenance. This may not always be so, because mechanization is being more and more successfully applied to library systems.

CIRCULATION OBJECTIVES OF VARIOUS TYPES OF LIBRARIES

Public, college and university, and special libraries differ in their objectives, because the clienteles and purposes served by these libraries and their parent organizations differ. Most important to public libraries are the circulation functions of:

1. Identification of materials charged out.
2. Identification of the borrower.
3. Obtaining the return of overdue materials.
4. Making a total count of items charged out.

Also desired by public libraries, but of less importance, are:

5. Adequate records of delinquent borrowers.
6. An efficient reserve (or "hold") system.
7. Detailed statistical information about books and readers.

College and university libraries generally feel that the most important circulation functions are items 1, 2, 3, 4, and 6, with items 5 and 7 also being desirable but less important.

Special libraries regard items 1, 2, and 6 of primary importance, with item 7 and an additional feature, library clearance of borrower, being desirable. The latter is accomplished by maintaining an additional file of charged-out material arranged by borrowers' names for use in the event a borrower leaves the organization.

CHARACTERISTICS OF CIRCULATION SYSTEMS FOR VARIOUS TYPES OF LIBRARIES

Public libraries feel that these features are most important in a circulation system:

1. Simplicity for public use and staff operation.
2. Economy in relation to total library budget.
3. Adaptability between branches and the central library.

Also desired, but of less importance, for public libraries are:

4. Adaptability for varying loan periods.
5. Minimal delay for the borrower in checking material out.
6. Minimal change-over costs and problems.
7. Ease of acceptance for return of books anywhere in a branch system.

College and university libraries consider items 1 and 2 most important and agree that 4, 5, 6, and 7 are also desirable. Special libraries, however, regard items 1 and 5 as most essential and consider items 2 and 6 as being next most desirable.

Consideration of the differences in objectives and operations of the various kinds of libraries will explain these choices.

CURRENT PRACTICES OF VARIOUS TYPES OF LIBRARIES

Larger public library systems are using transaction systems because of the cost savings, but college, university, and special libraries, which need book-location information at all times, use variations of the Newark system. The degree of borrower participation, i.e., his time and effort required in the circulation process, is greatest in college and university libraries, less in public libraries, and least in special libraries. Special libraries, in fact, usually permit material to be charged out by a messenger or from a telephone request and do not require a borrower to personally sign for books.

The loan period is usually uniform in a public library, varies according to the borrower (student or faculty) in a college or university library, and is often indefinite in a special library that tries to cater to the specific needs of individual members of its clientele. Fines are charged for overdue books by public, college, and university libraries (except not to faculty members) to encourage borrowers to return materials within the loan period, but generally a special library, serving the staff of its own organization, does not charge fines. Thus a special library must use other means to obtain needed items back from its borrowers. These may include direct appeals to individuals, protests to supervisory and management personnel in extreme cases, and purchasing additional copies of items as a substitute for requiring the return of such items.

SPECIFIC CIRCULATION ACTIVITIES

Circulation duties in every library will include many of the following tasks:

Registration and identification of borrowers. The purpose of this activity is to establish the right to borrow library materials and to serve as a record of a borrower's identity. The public library usually needs detailed information, the college or university library can utilize existing student and faculty records, and the special library usually has a limited and well-known clientele. Library technicians can be of great assistance in helping a new borrower fill out the required forms and in explaining the library's arrangement and regulations to him.

Charging and renewing.

Maintaining circulation records. As mentioned earlier, the procedures will reflect a library's need for book-location information and, in special libraries, the need to inform a departing borrower of all the publications charged to him at that time.

Discharging (or "slipping") *items returned to the library.* The purpose, of course, is to clear the records of the charge.

Collating special materials. This is an examination of certain materials each time they are borrowed or returned. The purpose is to protect items of special value, such as rare books, films, phonograph records, and the like.

Sending overdue notices. The purpose is to obtain items kept beyond the loan period. Procedures vary and may include sending several notices, phone calls, messenger service, and even legal action, but all such procedures should be performed as a regular routine action. Special libraries, which do not ordinarily have the concept of an overdue book, often send reminder notices instead of overdue notices, asking borrowers either to return material or to indicate they are still using it.

Collecting fines. Its purpose should be only an incentive for prompt return of borrowed items and not a source of library income. The size of fines varies, being low in public libraries and generally non-existent in special libraries. Regardless of the system followed, careful accounting and record-keeping are required to assure that the funds are properly managed.

Handling reserves. To allow a requester to obtain an item charged out to someone else, this activity consists of placing a "hold" or "reserve" on the item, recalling the item from its present borrower, holding the publication when it is returned, and notifying the new requester that it may be picked up.

Routing periodicals. This is done mostly by special libraries for the increased convenience of use of these important sources of current information. Procedures vary; some libraries keep current issues in the reading room for a limited period of time before routing, others route them immediately upon receipt, and others route copies of the tables of contents rather than issues themselves. Often a library will use a combination of routing procedures, depending on the particular periodicals and requesters concerned.

Paging. This is the activity of obtaining desired items from the shelves upon request. Although paging may seem to be only a routine chore, it provides an excellent opportunity for a library assistant to learn the collection, its organization, and the interests of its users. Additionally a librarian can be assisted by an assistant calling to his attention any areas of the stacks that are overcrowded or disorderly, or by noticing publications that need binding or mending.

Collecting statistics. The purpose should be to measure past and present library activity as a guide to future planning. Statistics can be helpful in measuring growth or decline of use, in analyzing various categories of books and readers, in budgeting book funds and determining acquisition policies, in weeding little-used materials from the collection, and in many other ways. The usual method of collecting statistics is to count circulation daily, record the count on forms, and cumulate them periodically.

Maintenance of the Collection

The purpose of keeping the collection orderly is to increase its usefulness by increasing the ease with which items can be located. As discussed in Chapter III, there are usually different kinds of organization schemes used for different kinds of materials in any one library.

A basic policy decision that must be made for each library, and for each portion of a library's collection, is whether to have open or closed stacks. The development of the United States public library brought the open-shelf type of collection into prominence, perhaps because of the American belief that everyone should have a good education and should have ready access to information. Although open stacks provide a reader with the great advantage of unrestricted browsing, the practice causes many internal operational problems in the maintenance of the collection. Even so, open shelves are felt to be preferable to placing a barrier between a reader and his books. Closed stacks, available only to staff members, are used by some libraries and in certain departments of many libraries when it is felt that considerations of internal library efficiency or other factors outweigh an open access policy.

SPECIFIC ACTIVITIES OF MAINTAINING THE COLLECTION

Every library will be engaged in most of the following activities:

Shelving and filing. In contrast to paging, this is the activity of returning items to their proper places after use, so that they may be located again when desired. Accuracy is vital in this operation, since a mis-shelved item is, practically speaking, a lost item. When shelving, care of the collection should also be considered by careful handling and avoiding overcrowding on book truck or shelves.

Shelf reading. This is inspecting each item on the shelves to maintain them in correct order. The frequency of shelf reading will vary according to the kind of material and the amount of public use of various portions of the collection. There should, however, be a planned schedule so that shelf reading is done with regularity.

Improving shelf appearance. The major purpose of this activity is to increase a user's ability and desire to use the collection, but it has the by-product benefit of keeping the arrangement of the collection more orderly. A good shelver should stand books upright with their spines in line with the front of the shelf, shift books to the left side of the shelf, and use bookends.

Shifting. This activity is required to relieve overcrowded shelves or for a move to a new area. A major shift requires more planning than might be apparent at first thought and should include measuring the available shelving, estimating present and future space needs, setting the height of the shelves, correcting shelf labels and stack guides, avoiding interruption of service, and developing procedures for the removal, storage, and re-shelving of material.

Taking inventory. The basic purpose of an inventory is to become aware of missing items that must then either be replaced or have their records withdrawn. The usual procedure is to compare the shelf list against the materials on the shelf, noting the discrepancies, and then to check circulation records and other possible locations such as mending shelves, the bindery, new book shelves, book trucks, and "problem" shelves. After a thorough check for missing items, needed titles are reacquired, and the catalog records are removed for titles not replaced.

An inventory has important added benefits in that it can increase the inventory-taker's knowledge and familiarity with the collection, locate mis-shelved items, indicate items for discard, and reveal discrepancies in cataloging or in processing. Libraries vary as to the frequency of taking inventory, but in many larger libraries it is carried on as a continuous activity. The current trend, however, is to eliminate taking inventories because of their high cost.

Reading room maintenance. This activity is included here because it too has the purpose of achieving a desirable environment for a library user. Attention should be given frequently to the neatness, cleanliness, and orderliness of the reading room.

In summary, performance of maintenance duties on a library's collection, which may often seem to be drudgery, are in reality very important to the successful operation of a library. They make the use of the library more pleasant for the readers and staff alike.

Reference Work

In this discussion of reference work, individual reference books or tools will not be considered, since the intent here is the why rather than the how of library activities. Just as it is necessary to have a good grounding in the principles of acquisitions and cataloging, it is necessary to have an understanding of the professional principles of reference work—even though much of the work may not be within the scope of responsibility of a library technician. In most libraries reference inquiries are handled by a professional librarian, but as has been mentioned, a library assistant many times is the first point of contact with a library user and will naturally be the recipient of his questions.

A librarian generally approves of library assistants answering as many information-type questions as possible, but reference questions, which require greater experience and deeper knowledge of subject matter, should be turned over to a professional. The line between these questions is a most difficult one to draw and depends heavily on the judgment of a library assistant. Remember that reference service is one of the prime services of a library and one on which a user will be quickest to judge its over-all worth. It is not a poor reflection on an assistant to refer questions to a professional but rather is an indication of wanting to provide the best service possible.

POLICIES DEFINING THE REFERENCE SERVICE

Policies defining the scope of reference work are difficult to determine, for whenever restrictions are placed on the services of a library, it is done reluctantly. Sometimes, however, restrictions are necessary to benefit the clientele as a whole, even though some individuals may be inconvenienced.

It is usually necessary to define the group to be served. Generally, libraries try to give maximum service to their own clientele and thus must give relatively little to outsiders. Whenever service is refused on such grounds, however, a questioner should always be referred to another appropriate library for help.

Restrictions may also have to be placed on the kinds of service that can be given. For instance, in a college or university library it is usually more appropriate to direct students to sources of information where they may find the answers themselves, since it is usually an educational objective of the school to teach students to use the materials found in a library. Limitations may have to be placed on the depth of service rendered by placing a time limit on reference questions whose answers would require a great deal of searching, as in preparing a bibliography on a technical subject. A library may have to refuse to answer certain kinds of questions, such as those for contests or wagers. This latter is a difficult restriction especially for public libraries, which receive many such questions from their tax-paying supporters. In such cases, it is appropriate to direct a requester to sources where the information may be found.

No library has infinite resources, so each must place some limitations on its service to give the most service in accordance with its primary objectives. Such restrictions should be carefully and wisely chosen and instituted only when absolutely necessary.

DEALING WITH A REQUESTER

A librarian has two objectives in mind in discussing a question with a requester. The first is to establish cordial relations with him to obtain his confidence and cooperation. He must always be shown courtesy, respect, and understanding. He should be given the time required for personal attention to his individual needs and capabilities. As mentioned earlier, a library technician's efforts along these lines are of great assistance.

The second objective in dealing with a requester is to clarify the problem to facilitate its solution. Most requesters seldom state their specific question immediately but instead make an attempt at self-service by asking more generalized questions or by requesting a book they think will contain the answers. The experienced librarian will recognize such requests as being preliminary to the real question and, through conversation, will further restate and refine the question. Expert probing of this kind is a necessary art in reference work.

If a question proves to be a highly technical or specialized one, a requester himself may aid in its solution by explaining terms or discussing allied subject fields that may lead to an answer.

A general rule in reference work, in cases when an answer cannot be provided with the resources immediately at hand, is to always provide some lead to further information that might be obtained. Perhaps a requester can be referred to another library more likely to have such information or to someone to whom he can write or telephone. A "no" answer without any promise of further help is poor service.

SOURCES OF INFORMATION

Without discussing particular titles, general types of information sources can be identified.

Personal knowledge. This is used mostly for simple informational needs but should be used with caution in the interest of accuracy and reliability. Personal knowledge is quite adequate for direction-giving answers to inquiries.

Card catalog. This is probably the most-used reference tool in the library, since a very common type of question deals with a specific author, title, or subject. Good reference work is impossible without good catalog usage.

Guides and manuals. These contain information on how and where to find information in particular subject fields.

Bibliographies. These are lists of publications in specific fields. For some subjects, they are not useful unless up-to-date.

Indexes and abstracting services. Such tools are highly useful as comprehensive guides to the literature, both for current information and for retrospective searching. They are especially important in science.

Encyclopedias. They contain general information about a great many topics, with individual sections usually written by specialists. Some encyclopedias are updated by "continuous revision" wherein only a portion of the articles are rewritten for each printing.

Handbooks and almanacs. These "gold mines of information" are compilations of data and information collected together in single volumes.

Dictionaries. There are language dictionaries and subject dictionaries, which are used for meanings, spellings, pronunciation, and derivation.

Annuals. These contain the record of current developments in a particular field.

Directories. There are many biographical and institutional directories for information concerning individuals and organizations.

Other types. Any item in the collection can serve as a reference tool to answer a question.

Outside the library. If a question cannot be readily answered by a library's collection, it may be answerable elsewhere, so a good reference librarian learns to use the telephone, correspondence, and consultation with colleagues and specialists in tracking down information. Special libraries probably utilize outside sources more than other libraries do, not only because they have smaller collections but also because they are often under greater pressure to come up with answers.

HOW TO STUDY REFERENCE BOOKS

As time permits it is rewarding to take a reference book from a shelf and examine it closely. The typical reference book is not arranged for continuous cover-to-cover reading like other books but has a special arrangement to facilitate finding information.

Examine the title page for general information on the book's scope, its author and his qualifications, the publisher, and the date. The preface or introduction is important in giving details of scope, special features, limitations, and comparisons with related works. The text itself should be carefully examined for arrangement, form of entry, cross references, supplementary lists, indexes, appendices, and the selection and content of material. Good techniques of evaluation are to look up specific topics about which one has personal knowledge, or if the book is a new edition, to compare it with earlier ones.

PERSONAL QUALITIES NEEDED FOR REFERENCE WORK

Reference work requires the development of as many of the following qualities as possible:

1. A pleasant, courteous, and friendly manner to foster good relations with the clientele.
2. A good memory to recall facts and experiences.
3. Imagination to re-think a question in different terms.
4. Thoroughness to be able to exploit a reference tool completely.
5. Accuracy in keeping a careful record of sources searched and the terms used in a search and also in recording all details without error.
6. Persistency to keep after a problem until it is solved.
7. Observation to pick up unexpected clues.
8. Judgment, to evaluate information found, to know how much time to spend looking, and to know when to refer a question to someone else.

Reference work is one of the most important services in a library since it involves the library patron so closely. Library technicians should be helpful in answering inquiries, and with experience and close cooperation with the librarian, they can contribute much to the reference function.

Other Assistance to Readers

Orientation of readers. It is most helpful to make an effort to acquaint readers with the collection, its arrangement, and the kinds of assistance and services available. It may be done informally with individuals and by tours, films, courses, or lectures to groups.

Readers' advisory service. This consists of directing a reader to materials or portions of the collection likely to contain materials pertinent to his interests. In some libraries, this may be extended to planning a reading program for an individual, which is a professional duty requiring skill in bringing readers and approprate books together.

Assistance in use of reference tools. This can include explanations of the arrangement and usefulness of the card catalog and an introduction to the proper use of bibliographic guides in the reference room.

Abstracting and annotating. This consists of summarizing the content of publications so that a reader may quickly select desired items. Such summaries may be either indicative (just briefly telling what the item is about) or informative (giving details, results, and data). Public libraries often prepare annotations of their books; special libraries may prepare abstracts of publications received, including periodical articles and news items. This activity requires skill and training in knowing the readers and the subject matter thoroughly as well as in writing summaries. The job is usually performed by a librarian or a subject specialist.

Many commercial abstracting services that are subject-oriented are available, usually from professional societies. These services are also called current-awareness services.

Translating. This may vary from a rough translation of a title to a detailed translation of a technical report. In some libraries short translations are made by a staff member possessing such ability, and longer or more difficult translations are obtained from outside agencies.

Selective routing. This consists of calling items to the attention of individuals according to their interests. It is a highly individualized service and requires a detailed knowledge of reader interests and technical understanding of the material being received and scanned.

Photocopying. Making copies of periodical articles and portions of other library items by photoduplicating equipment is termed photocopying. Much of a library's materials is copyrighted and as such is subject to the copyright laws forbidding reproduction without the copyright holder's permission. Generally, however, libraries are permitted to make limited copies—usually only one—since it is done for legitimate research purposes and not for profit. Libraries follow the principle of "fair use," which is the policy set down by the Joint Libraries Committee on Fair Use in Photocopying. This policy is summarized as follows:

> "*Findings* [of the committee]:
> 1. The making of a single copy by a library is a direct and natural extension of traditional library service.
> 2. Such service, employing modern copying methods, has become essential.
> 3. The present demand can be satisfied without inflicting measurable damage on publishers and copyright owners.
> 4. Improved copying processes will not materially affect the demand for single copy library duplication for research purposes."

> "*Recommendations:* The Committee recommends that it be library policy to fill an order for a single photocopy of any published works or any part thereof. Before making a copy of an entire work, a library should make an effort by consulting standard sources to determine whether or not a copy is available through normal trade channels."

Library assistants generally are responsible for photocopying and should be aware of the laws involved and the library policy. Any doubt about photocopying should be referred to the librarian in charge.

Publications. These may include the preparation of reading lists or bibliographies on specific subjects, booklists covering recent additions to the collection, and guides to the library's resources and services.

Other graphic aids. These may include bulletin boards for various kinds of information, displays illustrating some portion of the library's resources or services, shelf labels in the stacks, direction signs in the stacks and reading rooms, guides to shelf arrangement, guides to the use of the catalog, and the like.

Public Relations

Good public relations are important to the library just as they are to any business firm—the user and the organization are important to each other. The image that the library is an effective, helpful organization with a pleasant environment, eager to provide a good service, is a product of good public relations.

The role of a library assistant's relationship to the public has already been described. As a library's main point of contact with a user, the library assistant should represent the best qualities of library service. In difficult situations, the library assistant should know when to come to his supervisor for assistance, especially in matters involving library policy.

TECHNIQUES OF DEALING WITH THE PUBLIC

To become acquainted with techniques of dealing with the public, several statements are given below that describe common situations likely to occur at the circulation desk or reference desk. These statements are intended to clarify ideas about service to and behavior toward a library's public and to exemplify the principles of good public relations. The reader here should attempt to formulate his own reactions and answers to each situation before checking on the possible solutions that follow.

SITUATION:

1. A borrower wants to charge out a reference or non-circulating book.
2. A requester asks for "some information on Washington."
3. A reader is having difficulty locating material in the card catalog.
4. A reader is about to leave the library with a book he has not charged out.
5. A requester says that a particular book he wants "is always out."
6. Two library users are carrying on a conversation in tones that might be disturbing to others in the room.
7. Difficulty is encountered in recalling from a borrower a book that is wanted by another requester.

8. A borrower says he has already returned a book for which he has just received an overdue notice.

9. A reader expresses irritation about a particular library regulation.

10. A reader asks why this library doesn't follow a certain procedure or system that is used in another library with which he is familiar.

11. A user says that the card catalog listed a book under an incorrect call number.

12. A borrower hands in a circulation slip or form that is not completely filled out.

POSSIBLE SOLUTIONS:

1. Explain the reason why a book is put on a reference shelf or is made non-circulating, e.g., because of its heavy usage, its value in answering reference questions, or because of some intrinsic value, as illustrations. Frequently special libraries allow reference material to circulate for limited periods, like overnight or over a weekend.

2. Clarify the question. Does the requester want material on George Washington, Washington State, or Washington, D. C.?

3. Seize opportunities of this kind to explain the use of the library. A card catalog can be a very puzzling maze for those unfamiliar with corporate authors, inverted subject headings, and peculiarities in alphabetizing. Frequently a library user will not ask how to locate information since he feels he probably should know how. A polite inquiry of "May I help you?" is generally all that is required to have such a reader eagerly present his problem.

4. A busy person who has problems on his mind, and possible answers in the form of a book in his hand, will sometimes forget to sign out a book. A polite inquiry about "helping him charge out the material" is usually all that is required. Good public relations dictate that an accusative tone of voice should not be used.

5. A reader frequently is familiar only with titles he has used in the past. Try to satisfy his need for information by substituting another publication, by checking in the card catalog under the subject. Be sure to enlist the aid of the reference librarian if difficulty is encountered, because it is poor public relations to turn away a library user with empty hands when there is very likely to be other material available.

6. Politely ask loud talkers to lower their voices so that they will not disturb others trying to work. Usually a reminder of this type is all that is necessary. It is unwise to insist on absolute silence in a library, for many individuals use the library for private work conferences where reference materials are right at hand.

7. If repeated notices have been sent to a borrower and he does not return a needed item, do not assume he is just being difficult. A personal conversation with him may reveal a continuing need for the material, in which case an additional copy should perhaps be added to the collection. This decision is the librarian's. Sometimes revealing who the second requester is will be advantageous in that they may both be work-

ing on the same project. Explaining that the library must consider the needs of all of its users and that cooperation is important for the welfare of the group may be effective. As a last resort it may be necessary to contact the borrower's supervisor, but this is not the way to win friends for the library.

8. Assume he is correct. Offer to check the shelves and incoming material. Only after being sure that the material is not in the library, should the borrower be contacted again.

9. Try to find out why the regulation is irritating. Perhaps a troublesome procedure today would be overlooked tomorrow after work pressure has been relieved. Perhaps the reader cannot see the reasoning behind a regulation, and a short explanation will reveal the logic. By trying to see the user's point of view, the proper approach to a complaint of this type will present itself.

10. Again explain the reasoning behind a procedure or lack of procedure within the library. Remember that the organization of which the library is a part exerts a strong influence on a library's policies, so that what is done in one library is not necessarily appropriate or even possible in another library. Perhaps the reader's suggestion is a good one that should be brought to the attention of the supervisor for consideration.

11. Do not place blame for errors or make excuses but rather thank the library user for calling attention to an error. He has done the library a favor. Make note of the error for correction as soon as possible.

12. Ask the reader to complete the form and explain why all the information asked for is important for the records.

The answers to the situations supplied above are not the only right answers. They are only suggested solutions. It may be that a library requires all questions on procedure, for example, to be referred immediately to the librarian in charge. However, several general points of technique can be summarized:

1. Show good judgment at all times.
2. Refer a library user to the librarian in charge if there is any difficulty which cannot be handled quickly and simply.
3. Try to see the reader's point of view.
4. Be eager to explain library procedures.
5. Exhibit good personal qualities.

TECHNIQUES OF USING THE TELEPHONE

Much of a library's business with its public is conducted by telephone, especially in special libraries. The same techniques that were discussed in the preceding section would apply to the telephone also. Politeness may be even more important over the telephone, since a requester may not be identified. Local telephone companies usually can supply booklets and films that explain well the techniques of proper telephone usage.

Recommended Reading

ASHEIM, Lester. Wake Up! It's Time for Your Sleeping Pill. *Library Journal,* vol. 85, no. 2, January 15, 1960, p. 190-4.

COLLISON, Robert L. *Library Assistance to Readers,* 4th ed. New York: Philosophical Library, 1963. 139 p.

FRY (GEORGE) AND ASSOCIATES, INC. *Study of Circulation Control Systems* (Library Technology Project Publication No. 1). Chicago: American Library Association, 1961. 146 p.

HUTCHINS, Margaret. *Introduction to Reference Work.* Chicago: American Library Association, 1944. 228 p.

JESSE, William H. *Shelf Work in Libraries.* Chicago: American Library Association, 1952. 80 p.

WALLACE, Sarah Leslie. *Patrons Are People; How to Become a Model Librarian,* rev. ed. Chicago: American Library Association, 1956. 48 p.

WINCHELL, Constance M. *Guide to Reference Books,* 7th ed. Chicago: American Library Association, 1951. xiii, 645 p. + supplements.

Glossary

This glossary is comprised of a selected list of terms chosen from the text as those most likely to be encountered by a library assistant. The definitions are based on the usage of the terms within the text and are not meant to be detailed or exhaustive. The glossaries listed in the Selected References section were consulted.

ADDED ENTRY—A catalog entry other than the main entry—title, subject, series, and so on.

AGENT—An individual or firm acting as a middleman in the library's acquisition of material, commonly used in connection with subscriptions, back-files, and foreign publications.

BACK-FILES--Numbers of a periodical preceding the current issue.

BLURB—A publisher's brief advertisement of items from his list.

CALL NUMBER—Letters and numbers indicating the location of a book on the shelves and distinguishing it from all others in the library. The call number is composed of the classification and the author number.

CASING—see COVER

CLASSED CATALOG—A card catalog arranged by subject classification.

COLLATION—That part of the catalog entry that specifies the volumes, pages, illustrations, and other physical characteristics in a book.

COPYRIGHT—Exclusive right granted by a government to publish a work during a specified number of years.

COVER—The outer covering of a book or pamphlet. This may be boards covered with cloth (as in bound books) or heavy paper (as in paperbacks).

CROSS REFERENCE—Reference from one subject or name to another.

DESCRIPTORS—Another name for subject headings, generally used in indexing technical reports.

DICTIONARY CATALOG—A catalog in which all cards are arranged in alphabetical order.

DIVIDED CATALOG—A catalog divided into two or more units, as, an author and title catalog and a subject catalog.

DROP SHIP—Material originally ordered from a jobber but sent directly to the library from the publisher at the jobber's request.

EDITION—The text of a book resulting from a single type-setting. Each new edition indicates a significant change in the text.

END-PAPERS—The lining papers of a book cover, that conceal the hinges and seams of the cloth covering.

EPHEMERAL MATERIAL—Material of only temporary interest or value.

FRONTISPIECE—An illustration facing the title page.

HANGING INDENTION—A catalog card form in which the main entry is a title entry at first indention, all subsequent lines being at the second indention.

HINGES—The cloth strips that hold covers to the body of the book.

IMPRINT—Publication information—publisher, place, date—generally found at the bottom of the title page.

JOBBER—A wholesaler who sells publications of various publishers to libraries or bookstores.

JOURNAL—A periodical issued by an institution, corporation, or learned society and containing news and reports of activities and work in a particular field.

KWIC—Key-word-in-context. A type of index.

LEAF—A single printed sheet, comprised of two pages of text.

LETTER-BY-LETTER FILING—Strict alphabetical arrangement by letters, regardless of their division into words.

MAIN ENTRY—The principal entry, usually the author entry, giving the most complete information about the book.

MICROFORM—A generic term for various microphotographic formats. These are generally in the form of 35mm microfilm, 4 x 6 microfiche, and 3 x 5 Microcards. These differ primarily in that Microcards are opaque positive prints and cannot be directly reproduced, while both microfilm and microfiche are negative films and capable of direct full-size reproduction.

MONOGRAPH—A book on a particular subject, complete in itself.

NYP—Not yet published.

OP—Out of print.

OS—Out of stock.

PAMPHLET—An unbound monographic publication of under 64 pages.

PATENT—An official government publication containing specifications of an invention, such as a machine, a process, an art, or a design.

PERIODICAL—A publication with a distinctive title intended to appear at regular intervals and to continue indefinitely.

PREPRINT—Advance copies of papers given at conferences, symposia, and other meetings.

PRO-FORMA INVOICE—An invoice received for checking and approval prior to receipt of formal invoice. It is never approved and forwarded for payment.

REPORT—A publication giving an official or formal record, as of some special investigation, of the activities of a corporate body or the proceedings of a governmental body. A TECHNICAL REPORT, which is now frequently encountered in special libraries, is a record of the current status of scientific research and development, usually funded by a federal agency.

REPRINT—Singly reprinted articles taken from periodicals.

RUN—A library's holdings of a periodical title.

"SEE ALSO" REFERENCE—A reference to another subject heading under which additional information may be found.

"SEE" REFERENCE—A reference from a subject or name under which no entries are listed to a subject or name under which entries are listed.

SERIAL—A publication issued in successive parts, usually at regular intervals, and intended to be continued indefinitely. The term "serial" is an inclusive term covering periodicals, newspapers, annuals, and so forth and is not to be confused with "series".

SERIES—Separate, independent works related to one another by subject or treatment, issued under a collective title.

SHELF LIST—A card catalog arranged by call number order—as the books are arranged on the shelves.

SIGNATURE—Part of a book composed of several leaves, made by folding one large sheet of paper. The number of pages in a signature will always be a multiple of four.

SPECIAL LIBRARY—". . . a collection of information materials, maintained by an individual, corporation, association, governmental agency, or any other organized group, and primarily devoted to a special subject and offering specialized service to a specialized clientele. Special subject departments of universities and public libraries and of the Library of Congress shall be considered special libraries."

SPINE—The back-edge of a book that covers the stitching and usually carries the author and title.

STANDING ORDER—Order for a serial publication or subject classification specifying that each part be delivered as published.

STITCHING—Sewing holding the sections of the body of a book together.

SUBJECT HEADING—A term used to describe the subject content of a publication, taken from an authoritative source.

TECHNICAL REPORT—*see* REPORT

THESAURUS—Dictionary of terms generally used in cataloging technical reports; a subject heading list.

TILL-FORBID ORDER—Subscription order indicating that the periodical title is to be automatically renewed until cancelled.

TITLE PAGE—The identifying page of a publication, giving the author, title, edition, publisher, place, and date of publication.

TRACING—Record of all catalog cards made for one publication. This record is found on the main entry or shelf-list card.

TRADE BOOK—In general a book published by a commercial publisher as opposed to those published by societies, institutions, governmental agencies, and other non-commercial groups.

WEEDING—Selective discarding of library materials.

WORD-BY-WORD FILING—Arrangement word by word, alphabetized to the end of each word. Also known as "nothing before something."

Selected References

Directories

American Library Directory. New York: R. R. Bowker, 1908-.
  Biennial. Latest, 25th ed., 1966.

ASH, Lee, comp. *Subject Collections: a Guide to Special Book Collections and Subject Emphases as Reported by University, College, Public and Special Libraries in the U. S. and Canada,* 2nd ed. New York: R. R. Bowker, 1961. ix, 651 p.

Bowker Annual of Library and Book Trade Information. New York: R. R. Bowker, 1955-.

KAISER, Frances E., ed. *Translators and Translations, Services and Sources in Science and Technology,* 2nd ed. New York: Special Libraries Association, 1965. 214 p.

KRUZAS, Anthony Thomas, ed. *Directory of Special Libraries and Information Centers.* Detroit: Gale Research Co., 1963. 767 p.

Glossaries

AMERICAN LIBRARY ASSOCIATION. Editorial Committee. Subcommittee on Library Terminology. *A. L. A. Glossary of Library Terms, with a Selection of Terms in Related Fields.* Prepared by Elizabeth H. Thompson. Chicago: American Library Association, 1943. viii, 159 p.

MORLEY, Linda Huckel. *Contributions toward a Special Library Glossary,* 2nd. ed. New York: Special Library Association, 1950. 22 p.

TURNER, Mary C. *The Bookman's Glossary,* 4th ed., rev. & enl. New York: R. R. Bowker, c1961. viii, 212 p.

Miscellaneous

COLVIN, Laura C. *Cataloging Sampler: A Comparative and Interpretive Guide.* Hamden, Conn.: Shoe String Press, c1963. 368 p.

HISS, Sophie K. *A. L. A. Rules for Filing Catalog Cards.* Chicago: American Library Association, 1942. 109 p.

KRUZAS, Anthony Thomas. *Special Libraries and Information Centers: a Statistical Report on Special Library Resources in the United States.* Detroit: Gale Research Co., 1965. 42 p.

REDMAN, Helen F., and GODFREY, Lois E., eds. *Dictionary of Report Series Codes.* New York: Special Libraries Association, 1962. vi, 648 p.

WINCHELL, Constance M. *Guide to Reference Books,* 7th ed. Chicago: American Library Association, 1951. xiii, 645 p.
  Supplement, 1950-1952, 1954. 134 p.
  Supplement, 1953-1955, 1956. 117 p.
  Supplement, 1956-1958, 1960. 145 p.
  Supplement, 1959-1962, 1963. 151 p.

Index

Terms defined in the Glossary are not repeated in the Index.